It's not always easy to live happi... ......
Besides dealing with your own feelings about your situation,
you are often pressured by well-meaning colleagues, family,
friends, and members of your church. *Soloing* is a practical,
positive book on living life as a single Christian woman.
Laced with Luci Swindoll's enlightening insights and candid
recollections, this book presents comforting counsel and
creative ideas for coping with the social, sexual, spiritual,
emotional, and psychological aspects of being single. You'll
receive pertinent advice, written from a Christian perspective, on such areas as child raising, loneliness, sexuality and
the single parent, studying the Bible, and developing your
career. Authors include Virginia Watts Smith, Joyce Landorf, Jim Smoke, and Gary Collins. If you need encouragement and direction for dealing with the daily opportunities,
problems, and challenges you encounter as a single woman,
you will find the sensitive counsel you need in *Soloing*.

Soloing

Edited by
Luci
Swindoll

Power
Books

Fleming H. Revell Company
Old Tappan, New Jersey

Scripture quotation identified AMPLIFIED is from the Amplified New Testament © The Lockman Foundation 1954, 1958, and is used by permission.

Scripture quotations identified KJV are from the King James Version of the Bible.

Scripture quotations identified MLB are from THE MODERN LANGUAGE BIBLE—THE NEW BERKELEY VERSION IN MODERN ENGLISH, Copyright 1945, 1959, © 1969 by Zondervan Publishing House, and are used by permission.

Scripture quotation identified NASB is from the New American Standard Bible, © The Lockman Foundation 1960, 1962, 1963, 1968, 1971, 1972, 1973, 1975, 1977.

Scripture quotations identified NIV are taken from the HOLY BIBLE: NEW INTERNATIONAL VERSION, copyright © 1978 by the New York International Bible Society. Used by permission of Zondervan Bible Publishers.

Scripture quotations identified RSV are from the Revised Standard Version of the Bible, copyrighted 1946, 1952, © 1971 and 1973.

Scripture quotations identified TLB are taken from *The Living Bible*, Copyright © 1971 by Tyndale House Publishers, Wheaton, Ill. Used by permission.

Excerpts from the Super Guides are reprinted by permission. TODAY'S CHRISTIAN WOMAN, Old Tappan, N.J.

Quotations from *Open Windows* by Philip Yancey © 1982, used by permission of Crossway Books.

"Single Parents: Keeping Your Family Intact" is used by permission of the author, Elizabeth Hormann, Books Editor for *Single Parent* magazine and contributing editor to *Mothering* magazine.

Excerpts from *Changepoints* by Joyce Landorf copyright © 1981 by Joyce Landorf. Published by Fleming H. Revell Company.

Excerpts from *Suddenly Single* by Jim Smoke copyright © 1982 by Jim Smoke. Published by Fleming H. Revell Company.

Excerpts from *Single* by Marilyn McGinnis copyright © 1974 by Fleming H. Revell Company.

Excerpts from *Getting Started* by Gary R. Collins copyright © 1984 by Gary R. Collins. Published by Fleming H. Revell Company.

Excerpts from *The Single Parent* by Virginia Watts Smith copyright © 1976 by Fleming H. Revell Company; © 1983 by Virginia Watts Smith.

Diligent effort has been made to secure permission for all copyrighted material used in this book.

Library of Congress Cataloging in Publication Data
Main entry under title:

Soloing: experiencing God's Best as a single woman.

"Power books."
1. Single women—Religious life—Addresses, essays, lectures. I. Swindoll, Luci, date.
BV4527.S64   1985   248.8′432   85-2180
ISBN 0-8007-5194-9

Contents

PART THREE
KEEP PATCHING: In Tune With Our Sexuality

PART FOUR
LOOK ALIVE: In Tune With God

Bergie's Tunes

Luci Swindoll Reflects on Soloing

Her name was Bergendahl. Florence Bergendahl, and I'll never forget her. We called her "Bergie."

It was September 1950, and I had just turned eighteen. I arrived on campus about midafternoon—a greenhorn freshman, not yet dry behind the ears—with my earthly belongings in the car and a lilt in my spirit for what lay ahead. I was now a college student, a voice major, and my faculty adviser was Florence Bergendahl. She was head of the vocal department and little did I realize then what a tremendous influence she would have on my life. Immediately, everything about her fascinated me. She was tall, with a somewhat majestic presence, and even at the age of sixty she had perfect posture, a purposeful stride, and a booming voice. "So you want to sing, Lucille . . . you want to be a soloist?" she said to me upon our initial encounter. "Well, we'll see about that. Generally, in life, people do what they want if they want it badly enough. In time, we'll see how badly you want it." Right off the bat I was her captive audience.

You see, I had already met with this philosophy of life, ". . . people do what they want if they want it badly enough," from my father. Having grown up with the teaching that "if anybody else can do it, you can do it, too," when I heard that becoming a soloist was, at least in part, the logical progression of positive thinking, it made sense to me. And Florence Bergendahl was one positive thinker! I well remember arriving at her office for my early-morning voice lessons. No matter what kind of mood I was in, she was always on

7

top of the world. She would greet me at the door of her vocal studio with a warm spirit, often a joke or two (laughing heartily at her own punch lines), and escort me into the inner sanctum sanctorum of a room that made my eyes pop: enormous, shiny black grand piano with an immense drawing of Gustav Mahler hanging above it. Mahler, that nineteenth-century musical prophet of doom, looked as though he would cast both teacher and student into hell if a wrong note were sung in his presence.

There was a tailored sofa in front of a built-in bookcase, lined with volumes of all topics, and a large, austere desk covered with neat stacks of paper and musical scores. In the midst of those surroundings with that dynamic teacher I experienced mixed emotions. One side of me thought, *How miserable, how paltry is the life I lead by comparison to this person of vast musical wealth and culture. I should live differently—I should be different to merit the right to be in this room or be taught by this woman.* And the other side thought, *I love this. What a wonderful feeling I get in here. This is high cotton! I'd better learn all I can 'cause Bergie will kill me if I don't, and if she doesn't, Mahler will.* So, in that environment, in between the penetrating eyes of those two giants, Bergendahl and Mahler, I got my first taste of what it means to solo.

Bergie had pet phrases, short homilies by which she lived and which, I suppose, she imparted to all her voice students. While they occasionally sounded like orders, barked from the resonant hollow cavity of a top sergeant, they were meant as loving but firm teaching aids. "Straighten up," she'd say. "Never slouch. A good soloist stands tall and gets down to business. She gives herself to the music without holding back because she knows that's all there is at that moment. Think about that. Straighten up and give it your all. Get down to business." Getting down to business meant your eyes were straight ahead, your shoulder to the wheel, your ear to the ground, and your nose to the grindstone. It meant that in order to succeed, singing was not only pleasure but hard work as well. It was commitment to what mattered most and it meant cutting out the funny business when it was time to sing.

Now, don't misunderstand me. Bergie loved to have fun. She was not all work and no play. On Saturdays, for instance, she'd turn up the Metropolitan Opera Radio afternoon performance full blast and while the strains of that luscious music wafted across the airwaves of her room (and every other room in the teachers' dorm), she'd putt golf balls the extent of the fifty-foot hallway outside her door. When that little white ball entered the tilted cup at the far end, she would gleefully laugh and heartily, with full voice, join into the singing of the soloist or chorus at that moment in the radio music. No matter the voice range. No matter the opera. What mattered was that she knew them all by heart and she derived simultaneous pleasure from a hole in one and the thrill of being a tiny part of that splendid, timeless, universal music. Or, being an avid reader, Bergie insisted that all of us among her acquaintances read daily, as well. She would find an interesting or humorous article in the *New York Times,* discuss it at the dinner table, and ask each of us in her presence what we thought of the article. Did we learn any new words? Did we agree with its premise? If not, why not? Comment. Elaborate. Be definitive. "Oh, we're having fun now," we'd mutter to one another.

God help you if you went to your voice lesson without practicing or knowing your music. You'd need all the help you could get! "How do you think for one minute you can learn if you don't study, Lucille? Where *is* your music, under your bed? Get it out. Look at it. Memorize it. Practice it every day and make it part of you. You'll *never* be the singer you hope to be if you don't learn your music." I heard this many times during my lessons and rarely was there a time when Bergie assured me I had memorized deeply enough.

Because I was singing in Italian, German, or French, just to pronounce the words correctly wasn't good enough. What did they mean? Why did I think the composer or the librettist chose that word instead of another? How did the vowel sound in the word being sung match that particular note of the scale? Why were those specific dynamics or nuances used at that moment? Questions. Questions. Questions. Questions. *Gimme a break!* But, this woman wanted answers. She wanted to know what I thought. She wanted me to recognize the value of researching the music. She wanted me to be aware of the fact that singing a solo was a great deal more than repeating a series of black notes off a white page. Soloing was thinking for oneself.

Well, needless to say, after a few months of voice lessons from Florence Bergendahl, she became my beloved pedagogue and I became her devoted student and admirer. Everything in her life spoke of what I wanted to be. In my mind, I wanted her to be the mature version of the immature me. Once, she invited me to have breakfast in her dormitory apartment. Since I wasn't there for a lesson, we actually visited and I was able to see firsthand how she lived. The walls of her tiny rooms were literally covered with paintings and memorabilia she had collected on her varied travels throughout Europe. She had lived there for a period of time, singing professionally. In her inimitable way she told me bits and pieces about her fascinating life and, of course, I hung on every word.

For instance, she recounted the time she discovered a lump in her breast which, upon examination by a doctor, turned out to be a malignancy, resulting in a radical mastectomy. She was living alone at the time, and had very little money to pay for the surgery. In answer to my inquiry "How did you manage?" she said, "Well, you just trust God with your life, child. You call the hospital, set up a room for yourself, tell the doctor you hope he knows his business, and go have your surgery. After all," she went on, "if your faith doesn't work when the chips are down, and you never use it . . . what good is it?" So be it!

Bergie also told me about the months of private anguish she bore after the man she loved was killed in an automobile accident and her hopes and dreams for a life with him were shattered and fell all around her. "Slowly, no matter how numb you are, you pick up the pieces and patch them together. One hour at a time. One day at a time. And you wait for time to start its healing process. Finally, you come to life again. You go on with what you have."

I said, "Miss Bergendahl, how could you do that? If somebody I loved with all my heart died, I'd never want to sing again. I wouldn't want to live. How did you even have the emotional energy to sing? How did you find the desire?" She paused for a minute and looked very deeply into my eyes. Then she said the most interesting thing: "In the long run, I think that such a loss makes you a better singer. You learn what it is to let hurt work through your heart, and through your life ... and certainly, through your music. You know, Lucille, your singing reflects all that you are inside: your joys, your sorrows; your gains, your losses; your fullness, your emptiness. Life is like a patchwork quilt, and until you die, you'll keep patching."

Bergie's favorite expression was "Look alive! Nobody wants to watch a dead person sing. Remember, your voice is *you*, so smile. Sing. And look alive."

I graduated from college in 1955 and ironically, that same year Bergie retired from teaching voice. The evening of my senior voice recital, just prior to graduation, Miss Bergendahl gave me a lovely present: two books from her personal library; books I had repeatedly taken off her shelf and admired many times as I leafed through them. One was *An Anthology* by Albert Schweitzer and the other was *An Autobiography* by Frank Lloyd Wright. Bergie had had the good fortune to meet each of these men in the course of her travels and the latter book was autographed to her by the famous architect himself. Today I treasure these books as two of my most cherished belongings. Each book is a written account of the lives of men who made enormous contributions to history in general, and certainly to my life in particular. "This gift is to express my love for you," Bergie said as she handed me the present. "You've come a long way and I'm proud of your accomplishments. You sang a beautiful recital tonight. You got down to business!"

Ten years later, and for the last time, I saw Bergie again. I had been invited back to my alma mater to solo during the Charter Day homecoming festivities. She was there, too, and we had a touching, sweet reunion after those years of absence from each other. We talked nonstop about everything. Her life. My life. The world. Music. Traveling. The times in which we lived. And—I can recall it so vividly—just as I was about to walk onstage to sing before that gathered audience of old friends, Bergie looked at me, squeezed my hand, and said, "You're going to solo today my dear, so look alive." It was a *great* encouragement to me, and I sang that solo with all my heart. I sang it for her, if for no one else.

About a week later, in the mail, came a note from my friend and teacher, Miss Bergendahl. I still have it. I treasure it ... much like those two books she gave me so many years ago. Here is my favorite paragraph from that note:

> Your voice is beautiful my dear—more resonant and richer in quality. The Saturday morning solo was a delight—everyone listened with genuine pleasure. I watched their faces.

That was twenty years ago, and in one way or another, I've been soloing every day since.

To solo does not only mean singing without a partner. It means *living* without a partner. It means "going it alone." In the broadest sense, soloing is living a style of life where the work, the decisions, the plans, the actions are all done by oneself, the soloist. As I said earlier, soloing is thinking for oneself. There may be others in my life, in the same classroom, office, or home, but I'm not married to them. I'm not married to anybody. In the human capacity, I am alone. How am I going to handle it? How am I going to manage when the morass of life's problems presses in upon me and I feel I can't make it by myself?

Well, this book deals with some of those very struggles. It attempts to define, then address, some of the distinct complexities of today's person without a partner. And, in reading it, you will see how Bergie's principles for singing without partners carry over into living without partners. Let me show you what I mean.

Never Slouch: In Tune with Ourselves

In Part One, *Soloing* looks at getting in touch with ourselves. It encourages us to incorporate a program for living, whereby we become aware of our problems, seek to clarify them, and set about to stand tall in the midst of them, undefeated. "Never slouching" implies the refusal to allow our circumstances to immobilize us, coupled with the determination to rise above that which makes us low. Simply put, it is the picture of a person who faces the challenge of difficult conditions with the inner assurance of victory.

That sounds nice, doesn't it? It sounds like something we'd all like to achieve all the time, whether we're married or single. To view life's experiences as a constant winner is the ideal mental attitude. But, keeping in mind the fact that that which is ideal is rarely achieved, let's look at the next best picture—a framework in which we can actually live—reality. Reality conveys a very important truth. *Stop expecting something perfect!* I would say this precept is number one in getting in tune with ourselves and the first chapter of this book deals with that particular thought. I love the paragraph you'll be considering which says:

> At first glance, saying that God is with you when you're lonely may seem a little impractical when what you really want is a warm body next to yours. But if there isn't a warm body next to yours, you'd better get acquainted with whatever is in second place. And through the experience you just might discover that second place is better than first. God never lets you down. . . .

Often, we think it would be ideal to have a partner, but the author of chapter 1, Marilyn McGinnis, informs us that what may appear to be perfect in fantasy is never perfect in reality—because there is no perfect reality. Marilyn is saying, "Get acquainted with reality—it can be better than you think." Certainly not bad advice, and I've lived long enough to tell you it's the truth.

To be in tune with ourselves also means to develop inner resources. Marilyn goes on to say, "The wider your interests the less chance you have to be lonely." Hear, hear, and Amen! Let me add a tad more to that sentence, please: "The wider your interests the less chance you have to be lonely and the less chance you are to be boring." Oh! May God deliver us from boring people. Personally, I think boring individuals should be lined up and shot. I *hate* to be bored and if ever, *ever* I bore you, please stop me dead in my tracks, and suggest I listen to my own message of what should happen to those who bore others. Don't ever doubt it—diversification of interests and activities *always* makes a person more interesting and more interested in other people. It keeps down "bore pollution." I have often thought that one reason I so loved Bergie was she never bored me. She constantly challenged me to think for myself, to read, to grow, inquire, to be committed to music, people, and the fine art of living fully. Not a day passed during my college years that she did not challenge me to do that. And, needless to say, I am so glad she did because seeds were planted in me that will go on being cultivated until the day I die. So what if she was a bit off the wall or unorthodox in her behavior! I loved it. The more the merrier. The greater and more exciting the risk to live fully. She spoiled me for the average teacher and by simply being herself, she made me want to be better than I was. Because she never bored me, it made me want to improve myself so I'd not bore her.

Another interesting aspect of getting in tune with who we are is to envision ourselves through the eyes of other people, then—as chapters 2 and 3 point out—to face what we see there. As a preview, ask yourself some of these innocent-sounding little questions:

> Why do I always insist on my own way?
> What is it about commitment in a relationship that scares me so much?
> When I am defensive in a confrontation, what does that say about me?

In confrontations in my own life, for instance, I have watched a pattern emerge. As much as I personally hate them—hate to be confronted as well as hate to confront—when that act is conducted in love, it does more toward inner growth than almost anything else in my life. Please note, however, it's not the confronting that effects successful growth in a person—it is the fact that it's done "in love." *That* makes all the difference!

I challenge you to dig deep into your own reservoir of uniqueness and individuality. Search out new areas of understanding about yourself, create stimulating opportunities for expansion of interest or taste, and try very hard to open up to other people, investigating new and fun possibilities for outreach. You'll be so glad and so much richer when you do. There's never reason for a soloist to slouch. Be encouraged by this comforting verse in Romans 5, from our single friend the Apostle Paul:

For because of our faith, he has brought us into this place of
highest privilege where we now stand, and we confidently and
joyfully look forward to actually becoming all that God has had
in mind for us to be.

Romans 5:2 TLB

Learn Your Music: In Tune With Our Life-Style

In a very real sense, learning the music for the soloing life-style is
an ongoing, day-after-day, year-after-year responsibility. As my
friend Joyce Landorf says in the Prologue, just about the time you
think you have the music learned, somebody changes it. How true!

In the chapter "New Career Beginnings," you're going to see a
paronamic view of several avenues that will help you work through
the fears and frustrations of facing a change of jobs or, worse, going
back to work after being out of the job market for several, even
many, years. Jim Smoke also encourages each of us who is presently
employed to keep our talents and skills sharpened, honed, and
ready for action. An excellent idea.

Isn't that exactly what Bergie suggested when she said, "Where is
your music, under your bed? Get it out. Look at it. Memorize it.
Practice it every day and make it a part of you. You'll *never* be the
singer you hope to be if you don't learn your music." And . . . you
will recall, my hearing that only once was not enough. She drilled it
into me. I needed that admonition practically every voice lesson,
because somehow I'd get preoccupied with other things, go off on
various "toots," get lazy, and simply not work at singing well. But
she was always there to remind me that skills, talents, and abilities
require constant use and attention to run smoothly and be effective.
The more we practice, the sharper the skill! I like the way Jim
Smoke says it:

Investigate all the opportunities. Let yourself get excited! . . .
Many older singles seem content to serve time. Their unhappiness
and lethargy is largely due to their lack of motivation and belief
in themselves. Age has nothing to do with growth. New opportunities come to open minds and open hearts.

Bergie would have loved Jim Smoke. He was her kind of man!

Then, right on the heels of Jim's encouraging words, you'll come to a wonderful chapter about career building by Gary Collins. He introduces four prominent tunes of hope that ought to put any off-beat soloist back into the rhythm of living. Simple to sight-read? Yes. Easy to sing? No. Gary, however, presents many sound ideas and rational judgments for how to make his concepts work, and all that he tells us makes good sense in building a career. He even spends some time on the importance of mentors. In my words, he asks if there is anyone in your life doing for you what Bergie did for me. Let's go one step further: are you a mentor for anyone else?

At this point, let me digress from the contents of this book for a moment and tell you something about my own career as a single woman. Since I have recently become an executive with the Mobil Oil Corporation, it is amazing how often I am asked the same series of questions:

> How did you get there?
> What is your secret to success?
> How many years does it take to become a manager in a large corporation?
> What would you advise the young person who wants to be in your shoes someday?
> Is being an executive gratifying or just a lot of hard work?

Let me answer that double whammy in the fifth question first, then I'll move into the condensed version of Swindoll's Management Moves. Yes, being an executive (for me, anyway) is extremely gratifying. It is a whole new way of thinking and it is a level of responsibility and concern that calls forth my deepest degree of judgment, balance, knowledge, and every shred of wisdom I can muster. It keeps me on the cutting edge of life and forces me to think cogently. Being an executive makes one accountable and humbled at the same time; it is a simultaneous reliance upon one's own inner resources and upon the assurance of God's constant provision and direction. I love it because it causes me to reach higher and deeper all the time. And, yes! It is a lot of hard work. But, it's fun, too. As I have said for years, one of my favorite activities in life is doing something constructive while having a good time. To me, that's what being a manager and an executive is.

But, more important, permit me to look at those other questions for a minute. There are no concrete answers to any of them because they are abstract and, for the most part, my responses would be relative to my own particular temperament, personality, and working style. Generally speaking, however, success is not a state of being as much as a process. There is no formula that, when applied at the proper time, leads one unfalteringly up the ladder of success. Many factors enter into what makes a successful employee and (for that matter) person, I believe. But there are two ingredients which, in my way of thinking, play a huge part in the majority of success stories. I have found that these ingredients are not only applicable to one's career but to the single life-style as well. And it is amazing how simple the principles are, yet so difficult to apply. First: *be patient with yourself!* Keep reminding yourself that that which is valuable is not achieved in twenty minutes, or a day, or overnight, or even in a year. Nothing of value comes suddenly. I cannot improve upon the words of the author Dashiell Hammett, who wrote:

> That big hour of decision, the turning point in your life, the some-day you've counted on when you'd suddenly wipe out your past mistakes, do the work you'd never done, think the way you'd never thought, have what you'd never had, it just doesn't come suddenly. You trained yourself for it while you waited—or you've let it all run past you and frittered yourself away.

That's what I mean about success being a process. "You trained yourself for it while you waited. . . ." Success comes by hanging in there over the very long haul.

Second, and with the same degree of emphasis, I would say: *learn to defer rewards.* When you plan your objectives, your goals, or your life, allow room for realistic postponements. Keep anticipating. Imagine your future the way you want it to be, then prepare to shift gears along the way in arriving at the realization of that future. Quit having to have it all *now!* As Gail Sheehy, in her marvelous book *Pathfinders,* reminds us:

> To the degree that we learn to anticipate the future, we increase our control over the direction of our lives. As we know, the pri-

mary source of well-being is the conviction that one's life has meaning and direction. To arrive at that conviction—to weave the delicate web of love, work, family, purpose, and pleasure that might support a fully engaged life—depends to a considerable degree on the right timing. And to get the timing right demands that we train our powers to predict the future.

To be in tune with the life-style of the unmarried means to look at your life where you are now and where you hope to go with it. It implies making an honest appraisal of your schooling, career, and finances—all the demands that press in upon you from the outside—in light of your present objectives and your future goals. Again, the Apostle Paul states it much better than I can:

> This should be your ambition: to live a quiet life, minding your own business and doing your own work, just as we told you before. As a result, people who are not Christians will trust and respect you, and you will not need to depend on others for enough money to pay your bills.
>
> 1 Thessalonians 4:11,12 TLB

How's that for a practical principle for living?

Keep Patching:
In Tune With Our Sexuality

Of all the inquiries put before me in seminars with singles, probably the most prevalent are those dealing with one's sexual drives. Questions like, How is sex handled apart from marriage? Or, more commonly, If you've been married and know sexual satisfaction in that marriage, how can you get by without it for the rest of your life?

My first reaction is to say, "I don't know," and in most individual cases, I really *don't* know. Those are tough questions and the answers usually depend on the choices we want to make.

Remember the morning I had breakfast with Bergie in her dorm apartment? Do you recall her pearls of wisdom when I was incredulous that she could continue her career as a professional singer, having suffered the deep loss of the man she loved? "... your singing reflects all that you are inside," she said, "your joys, your sorrows; your gains, your losses; your fullness, your emptiness. Your life is like a patchwork quilt, and until you die, you'll keep patching."

Contrary to the public opinion of the majority, one's sexuality is not predicated upon how well one performs in bed. Sexuality "involves one's whole emotional being," Jim Smoke tells us in Part Three of this book. "It includes intimacy, love, feelings, consideration, kindness, caring, support, and trust. It is involvement with another person that is total and complete, and continues that way through life." Bergie is saying the same thing. Sexuality, in its deepest sense, is made up of many parts, patched together like a quilt, and we keep putting those different pieces of fabric together into that quilt until the work is finished and we're gone. Sexuality is a composite—the feeling, caring, tender, affectionate part of a person—that part of us which has the capacity to give and receive love. And, it is vital to life.

The very serious topic of sexuality for the person without a marriage partner is addressed in a credible and sensitive manner in this book. I respect each author's personal stand and advice, and I admire any individual in life who has the courage and conviction to live by Paul's admonition:

> Don't you realize that all of you together are the house of God, and that the Spirit of God lives among you in his house? If anyone defiles and spoils God's home, God will destroy him. For God's home is holy and clean, and you are that home.
>
> 1 Corinthians 3:16,17 TLB

Don't forget. This is a book about soloing through life. That means each of us can sing our songs of life in any key we choose—major or minor. But I can assure you from my own past experience and from the confessions I hear from other single friends, probably more discord can be rendered in this arena than in any other, if we elect to stay out of tune with our sexual expressions. Even though we all have the freedom to choose, let's not delude ourselves into believing that our sexual needs and their subsequent satisfactions, outside the bonds of marriage, will change the veracity of God's Word. It stands sure, and doesn't change.

Look Alive: In Tune with God

"Look alive," Bergie said. "Nobody wants to watch a dead person sing. Remember, your voice is you. So smile. Sing. And look alive." Not only was that her favorite expression but it was also my favorite expression *of* hers. It captured the essence of encouragement for soloing. In the same way, it captures the essence of effectual living. It puts the strength and power of living where it belongs—in the ability to effectively project one's inner resources, tranquillity, assurance, and vitality to the rest of the world. Looking alive is the "presence" that provides the soloist with the vehicle to convey his or her own individual personality and quintessence. It is the heart and kernal of attractiveness. It's not outward good looks; it's inward essence. It's not dependent upon clothes, hair, grooming, age, makeup, or weight. It is dependent upon character. Ah! Therein lies the real person, and that real person's beauty comes from being in tune with God.

There is much good information in Part Four of this book—information we singles need to know to help us rely upon God. You know, Bergie and the Apostle Paul should have known each other. I think that by now they do. When I read these words of Paul, I could not help but think those two lived by much the same philosophy:

> Christ rose from the dead and will never die again. Death no longer has any power over him. He died once for all to end sin's power, but now he lives forever in unbroken fellowship with God. So ... be alive to God, alert to him, through Jesus Christ our Lord.
>
> Romans 6:9-11 TLB

You're going to solo today. So, do it with confidence, resonance, vulnerability, and inner beauty. People will listen with genuine pleasure. You watch their faces. They'll be captivated. They will desire what you have. They, too, will want to look alive and get down to business. You show them how it's done.

Luci Swindoll

Prologue

From *Changepoints* by Joyce Landorf

It seems to me that there are at least two kinds of soloing. The musical soloing, where we sing by ourselves; and life-style soloing, where we live, sing, or cry by ourselves.

The musical kind I've known about all my life. And—while this next statement may not be terribly profound—let me tell you: Soloing wouldn't be all that nerve-racking except for the fact that somebody is always changing the music. Each piece that comes along is brand new, each song has a change of tempo and pace, and each musical rendition brings with it its own challenge.

I'm not too sure that life-style soloing is all that different from musical soloing. For about the time you adjust to living solo and you're getting the hang of it, someone or something changes the music. The cadence is off the beat, the lyrics overwhelm you. What can *never* happen—*does*. In one fell swoop your song is a jumbled-up bunch of discords and sour notes.

For many years I have traveled, written books, talked, and listened to many thousands of women. Many of those women are, for one reason or another, single. Some are soloing by their own choice; others, by uncontrollable circumstances, some by divorce, and still others by widowhood. But they are all living out this time in their lives on their own and by themselves.

Some of the most beautiful people in the world today, you may never have heard of. They've not written books, been on talk shows, nor are they household names. But they *are* beautiful and they are all *soloing*. There is a beauty in their lives that really shines. The glow from their heaven-sent contentment is simply breathtaking.

Thousands of women are soloing in our world today—the beautiful ones are the ones who have *chosen* to accept soloing as God's plan for now. Acceptance followed by contentment are the flags that fly above them!

Paul was single, and his wisdom, borne out of soloing, has come down through the ages. I'm glad he was single! Actually, he would most likely have made a poor husband and father. Can you imagine Mrs. Paul being asked the whereabouts of her husband? She'd have to say, "Oh, he's off cruising the Greek Islands." Or, when his son asked if his dad was coming home soon, his mother would have to answer, "I'm afraid not right away. He's in jail—again."

Oh, dear. Enough of this.

Paul was a soloing expert. In his letter to the Philippians he wrote about being ". . . satisfied to the point where I am not disturbed or disquieted in whatever state I am" (Philippians 4:11 AMPLIFIED). And then, in that same letter, he tells how he has managed to live in times of plenty or in times of want. Also in the Amplified Bible, it's beautifully put when Paul writes, "I have learned in any and all circumstances the secret of facing every situation. . . ." It seems to me that he examined all the alternatives open and *chose* the way he would face every situation.

I wish Paul had elaborated on the word *secret,* but I think he did give us a clue when he mentioned *facing* every situation.

Before we can adjust to life, as it is for us, we have to *face* it. Verbally or nonverbally we have to admit, "This *is* happening." For instance, one of the most positive steps out of the valley of bereavement comes when a widow says firmly to herself, "My husband is *not* coming home from the office or from a business trip. He will *not* hold me or his children in his arms anymore. I will *not* be able to hear his laugh or tease him about his funny way of sneezing. He is *not here* anymore. I'll see him in heaven, but *not* on this earth again."

By choosing to face up to this dreadful yet real fact, this woman can go about adjusting her thinking, her attitudes, and her responses. She can begin to plan again. It's solo this time, and maybe that's brand-new to her after thirty-some years of marriage, but it's *the way things are.* She now has a choice. She can accept and adjust to learning the secret of being content, or she can withdraw from family, friends, and the world around her. She can even harbor bitterness until its odious festering eats away her inner soul.

Many people, not just those soloing, suffer from the debilitating malaise commonly known as the "When and Then" syndrome. It sounds like this:

When I get married and find Mr. Right,
then I'll be happy.

When I have children,
then I'll feel fulfilled.

When my church gets a pastor I like,
then I'll get involved.

When my boss gives me a raise and I get some money,
then I'll tithe.

When my divorce is final,
then I'll be really free.

When I get my tax-refund check,
then I'll buy a new wardrobe and be beautiful.

When I succeed in my work,
then I'll get respect from my parents and others.

The trouble with the "When and Then" syndrome is that it forces you to live completely in the future. You miss today's new's and now's. Also, this kind of thinking sets your expectations too high and somehow—if you do find Mr. Right, if you do get a promotion, if you do succeed, et cetera, et cetera—the "then" is never what you dreamed it would be. You find yourself in the cold winter of disillusionment, and there you are shivering without a coat.

Someone has said, "The trouble with perfectionists is that they are never ready." Living continually in the future, with enormously high expectations, cripples you so you are never quite ready for the now's of your life.

Saint Paul wanted us to live in the "Now and How" of our lives, choosing to accept and being content with *whatever* state the now presents. The "Now and How" syndrome would read like this:

> Now I am living alone.
> How wonderful to know Jesus is *here with me.*

> Now I am divorced.
> How comforting to understand that God has not rejected me.

> Now I am a widow. (A darling older lady—recently widowed— actually said this when I asked her to find something to be thankful for. She showed the practical side of God when she said:
> How grateful I can be that on Monday nights I don't have to listen to Howard Cosell.)

> Now I am a single parent.
> How good it is to be assured that God is participating in my parenting.

> Now I've lost everything.
> How blessed it is to have the freedom of Christ to cry, feel broken, and know healing is on its way.

> Now I am a woman—soloing.
> How incredible of God to write Isaiah 54 as a love letter just to me!

The "Now and How" syndrome is beautifully expressed by Eugenia Price. I don't know where or when she said this—I found it among my papers on a scrap piece of pink paper. It reads, "The only direct statement of Jesus which is simple enough for me to comprehend when my heart is breaking, or when I'm discouraged or scared is: 'Follow me.' I cannot understand life because life is not understandable, but I can grasp, 'Follow me.' "

That is choosing to follow today. This moment. Not tomorrow or when it's convenient, but *now.*

Part One

Never Slouch: In Tune With
Ourselves

Aloneness is often confused with *loneliness,* but that's a lie we like to tell ourselves to dodge what might be the real problem. We could just be boring our listeners into unconsciousness. It need not be. Once we get a glimpse of the end-less possibilities for discovery and outreach, and start moving in that direction, we will begin to realize that the future is only as lim-ited as our imaginations, priorities, and ener-gies. We will also be a lot more fun to be around, and that is *very* important to being in tune with ourselves and liking ourselves. We'll stop slouching over the telephone, hoping it will ring with that hot invitation from Mr. Wonderful, because we'll simply be too in-volved with living.

1

Alone—or Lonely

From *Single* by Marilyn McGinnis

To be alone means simply that you are by yourself. It is a physical thing. Loneliness, on the other hand, is psychological. The lonely person may be surrounded by people, but he feels as if he is the only person in the world. "Loneliness," says William E. Park in *The Quest for Inner Peace,* "is when you are forced to be alone against your will; solitude is when, like Thoreau, you are willingly alone." Aloneness is positive. Loneliness is negative.

Consider for a moment some of the values of spending time alone. Sometimes you need to be alone just so you can catch up with yourself. If you've been burning the candle at both ends, stay home one night for a change. Turn on some soft music, take a leisurely bath, and hit the sack early. Rest and relaxation are an important part of staying healthy. Isaiah 30:15 (KJV) says that "in quietness and in confidence shall be your strength." Sometimes you can best achieve that strength when you are alone.

Just as your body needs rest and restoration, so does your mind. The psalmist said, "He leads me beside restful water; He revives my soul," (Psalms 23:3 MLB). Restoration of the soul takes place beside the restful waters, not in the hustle and bustle of activity. Creative use of your time alone provides the physical and mental strength you need to cope with the problems that face us all from day to day.

Where you spend your time alone is up to you. But it's interesting to note that the psalmist mentions the restfulness of water. How many times have you paused to watch a tumbling waterfall, felt the cool spray from a fountain, or studied your reflection in a shimmering pond—and wished you didn't have to leave? Some of my most restful moments have been listening to the waves lap against the shore at the ocean. I wouldn't dare live overlooking the ocean. The waves would mesmerize me and I'd never get anything done. If you're feeling extra tired, don't overlook the possibility of a weekend spent relaxing at a lake or the seashore.

Another value of spending time alone is the opportunity it affords us to find direction for our lives. Why are we here? What are we doing? Where are we going? These are important questions that each of us must answer if we are going to lead meaningful lives. Like the man who jumped on his horse and rode off in all directions, our lives sometimes become a mumbo jumbo of activity until we wonder if we're accomplishing anything at all. We try first one thing, then another, never satisfied with anything. The problem, perhaps, is that we've never spent time alone with ourselves thinking through what life is all about.

The only way you can truly find direction for your life, of course, is to spend time alone with God. As surely as He allowed you to be born, He has a plan for your life. He sent His Son to die that you might live. He provided a written Word to guide you step by step. He sent His Holy Spirit to comfort you and help you live God's way. But none of what God has provided will ever be a reality for you until you spend time alone with Him. Not time spent telling Him all your troubles. (Of course, He wants you to do that, too. He's called the Comforter for a reason.) But you must also spend time listening to Him speak to you. That's not something you do at a moment's notice. It takes time—alone.

Being alone also provides opportunity for you to develop your creativity. It isn't likely that the great music of Mozart or the poetry of Keats was written in the middle of a crowded room. I have an author friend who can write a book sitting in the living room of his home with a typewriter on his lap and the children playing nearby. But he's a rare one. Most of us need peace and quiet before the ideas start to come. You think you aren't creative? Maybe that's because you've never spent time alone to find out.

"But I'm So Lonely"

No matter how creatively we may use our time alone, however, there will be times when all of us feel lonely. Perhaps you have lost your husband through death or divorce, or recently broken an engagement to someone you truly loved. Until you are over the shock of separation, you will undoubtedly have periods of loneliness. Or perhaps you miss a special friend who is away. Occasional lonely moments are normal and inevitable. If we didn't *care* about people we wouldn't be lonely. I asked a group of single women to complete three sentences with the first words that came to mind: "Loneliness is . . ." "I feel lonely . . ." and "I feel lonely especially when. . . ." Some of the women defined *loneliness* as follows. Do you agree with their definitions?

Loneliness is:
self-centeredness
pity for oneself
inability to receive and give
not having a special someone to share with
wanting to be with someone and being alone
not knowing Christ as your Saviour
isolation from loved ones
a state of feeling regardless of who is around you
being and feeling unwanted
when you feel less important than the smallest star
an empty feeling
feeling sorry for yourself
being alone in a big city where you don't know a soul
needing people but afraid to call anyone for fear of being
    rebuffed
needing someone to need you
not being able to share yourself and your thoughts with
    someone who cares

Instead of *defining* loneliness, some women *reacted* to it. Have you ever felt the way they feel?

Do you feel that loneliness is:
  my own fault
  the lot of the single person
  my middle name
  unhealthy
  all around me
  depressing
  bearable but unpleasant
  probably the biggest thing single people fear
  frightening at times

Or do you see loneliness as:
  a battle but not limited to the single
  easily overcome if we would seek Jesus' face
  healthy sometimes—what I do with it is especially important
  miserable but perhaps makes you more appreciative of others
  beneficial when it enables one to be creative in her loneliness
    or as a result of the experience of loneliness
  different from being alone
  not a bad feeling—reminds one to turn to the Lord
  helpful in drawing closer to God
  the worst feeling one can have, but it can lead to spiritual
    growth and personal insight

For some people loneliness is a chronic problem. They are haunted by the feeling that nobody loves them, nobody cares.

Some people feel lonely because they do not have any close friends. They lack the social skills necessary to develop meaningful relationships with people and have no one to whom they can truly open up their hearts.

How close are you and your best friend? Are there people—both men and women—in whom you feel free to confide? Is there anyone whose shoulder you can literally cry on if you feel like it? If making friends is a problem for you, a competent counselor can help you discover what is preventing you from sharing yourself with others.

Look back at the definitions for *loneliness* listed earlier. Which of those definitions best sums up the basic cause of loneliness? If you chose "self-centeredness" you are quite right. Prolonged loneliness is the result of feeling sorry for yourself—in short, a preoccupation with yourself. Without realizing it, your innermost self may be saying, "Poor me. I've got nobody and nothing. If somebody else won't give me some attention I'll give it to myself. Poor, poor me." Or maybe you drag your "poor mes" with you wherever you go—using them as a device to get attention and sympathy. It may work for a while, but eventually people get tired of listening to other people's sob stories. Instead of getting attention, you may find people turning their backs on you altogether.

The woman who gives of herself to others has little time to feel lonely. The love that she gives to others is returned in abundance. Maybe your problem is that you aren't involved enough in service to other people.

The danger with prolonged loneliness is that it tends to lead to things that are worse. The pattern goes something like this:

You feel lonely. You wish you had a man. And so you think, *If only I had a man I wouldn't be lonely.*

The more you think about it the more depressed you become. The more depressed you become, the angrier you get.

Why don't *I have a man? Doesn't God like me? Why is He denying me the very thing I need most?*

Or maybe you get mad at yourself.

If I weren't so ugly (tall, short, fat, thin, stupid, intelligent), I would have a man. Nobody wants a dumb cluck like me.

The anger at yourself, others, or God leads finally to guilt, because you've always been taught that a Christian isn't supposed to get angry. And so the vicious circle continues.

Loneliness leads to depression, which leads to anger, which leads to guilt. No matter where you begin on the circle, one thing leads to another. Anger and unhappiness that were smoldering underneath suddenly ignite. The pattern is set and unless you take steps to correct it, it will develop into a life-style that lasts for years—perhaps all of your life.

What to Do When You've Got the "Poor Mes"

How can you overcome loneliness?

The first step is to put loneliness in its proper perspective. Nobody has a corner on loneliness, least of all you. Single people are lonely at times. So are married people. When you stop to think about it, what could be more lonely than living in the same house with someone who no longer loves you or someone you no longer love?

Listed below are some of the times when single women say they are most apt to feel lonely. As you read through the list, check those which apply primarily to single women, and those which apply to married women, and those which are a particular problem for you.

	Single Women	Married Women	Me
I feel lonely when:			
I have nothing to do	————	————	——
I am by myself too long	————	————	——
my friends are getting married	————	————	——
I'm around a lot of couples by myself	————	————	——
it's my birthday or a special holiday and I don't have a "special" man to share it with	————	————	——
I am not loved	————	————	——
I go shopping	————	————	——
I have my period, which might make me more aware of my desire for marriage and children	————	————	——
I feel I have let someone down	————	————	——
others are dating and I'm not	————	————	——
I'm physically tired	————	————	——
I've come close to dating a special guy and the date has fallen through	————	————	——

	Single Women	Married Women	Me
I see others enjoying family life			
I'm with a group of couples and I'm the only single			
viewing a beautiful scene alone			
I am selfish			
I think about the past and future			
I have decisions to make			
I can't be with men at least several times a week			
I have a disagreement with someone			
I am discouraged			
I'm with people with whom I'm not at ease			
I don't have a guy around whom I care for			
I feel I have failed in some important task			
I think of men I admire			
my roommate has a date or my friends have dates			
I think about the man I once loved			
in a crowd			
it's nighttime			
I sit around and think about it			
I can't see the reasons for what God is doing for me			

Be honest about your emotions. If you feel lonely or angry or scared, admit it. Only then can you deal with it constructively.

At the root of chronic loneliness is the feeling that nobody cares. But all you have to do is pick up your Bible to realize that Somebody *does* care. Jesus said, ". . . lo, I am with you alway, even unto the end of the world" (Matthew 28:20 KJV). The writer of Hebrews 13:5 (KJV) reminds us that God has said, "I will never leave thee, nor forsake thee." In John 15:13, 14 Jesus said, "No one has greater love than this: to lay down his life for his friends. You are My friends if you do what I command you" (MLB).

At first glance, saying that God is with you when you're lonely may seem a little impractical when what you really want is a warm body next to yours. But if there isn't a warm body next to yours, you'd better get acquainted with whatever is in second place. And through the experience you just might discover that second place is better than first. God never lets you down. God is always with you. God loves you—no matter what. God wants to give you only what is best for you. God's best gifts bring joy. God's shoulder is always ready for you to cry on. Now wherever could you find a better friend than that? Commit your loneliness to God and ask Him to remove it or use it for His glory.

Some situations that produce loneliness are predictable. Be prepared for them.

If you always drag bottom on Friday nights when you don't have a date, plan something exciting for the weekend. Don't resign yourself to a lonely evening at home.

If physical weariness or the beginning of your menstrual period are sure to produce a case of the "poor mes," recognize it for what it is. When the pangs of loneliness hit, remind yourself that the cause is largely physical and will go away of its own accord in a few hours or days.

Holidays are often difficult because they are usually family-centered. If you are away from your family you feel left out and alone. If a family whose friendship you enjoy invites you for the holidays, go and be your cheeriest self. Sometimes, however, people make you feel worse instead of better. I'll never forget the well-meaning lady at church who once invited me to Thanksgiving dinner and informed me that she was trying to round up the "strays" (or words to that effect) who had nowhere else to go. I made up my mind I would definitely have someplace else to go.

Another year I decided to become the master of my own fate. Instead of counting myself among the rejects, I invited a family to

Thanksgiving dinner with me at my apartment. Their oldest son had just entered the service and I thought *they* might be a little lonely without him. It was one of the happiest holidays I ever spent.

One of the definitions of *loneliness* listed earlier in this chapter was "needing people but afraid to call anyone for fear of being rebuffed." A friend tells me this was not a problem for her when she lived with someone, but became a problem when she lived alone. For example, she might want to call a girlfriend and ask if they could have dinner together, but she was afraid of being turned down. So she protected herself by planning alternate activities that she would also enjoy. At the top of the list would be having dinner with her friend. But if the friend had other plans, there were a couple of other activities she could fall back on and enjoy.

Look at the situations you've checked which are most apt to make you feel lonely. How many of those can you predict and plan for in advance?

While many situations are predictable, some are not. No matter how popular you may be, sooner or later you end up with an unplanned evening at home. A big date fell through at the last minute, your plans for a ski weekend ran amuck, or your car broke down on the way out of town, and you're stuck at home. Unless you have some inner resources to draw upon, such times can be disastrous.

If loneliness is about to set in, work five minutes at something—sewing, cleaning house, trying a new recipe—and it will usually get you over the hump. When asked what she does on Friday night, one girl replied, "Sometimes I cry and then I clean out my dresser drawers." At other times she loses herself in a good book and enjoys the evening alone. (By the way, there's nothing wrong with having a good cry once in a while. It may be just what you need to clear out the emotional cobwebs.)

The wider your interests the less chance you have to get lonely. Do you have any hobbies? Are you reasonably proficient at at least one sport? Now is a good time to develop some hobbies, learn a new language, improve your skills at sports, or volunteer your services at the church or some other service organization. Here are the ways some single women tell me they spend their free time:

volunteer hospital work

sponsor a youth group

organize, plan, and attend group social activities, Bible studies, prayer groups, dinner parties

refinish furniture

attend single adult functions

go to Christian socials that are on Friday and/or Saturday nights

read the Bible (do you have a plan for studying the Bible? Check with your local Christian bookstore for some books on how to study the Bible. Or take a course at a Christian college or Bible school. You can get hooked studying the Bible and the time will fly.)

play golf

go stag to school banquets and church affairs

go bowling

stay home and sew

catch up on needed sleep

The possibilities are endless, limited only by your own imagination.

My final suggestion is that you make your aloneness work for you. For example, you attend a party and you don't know a soul there. You feel terribly lonely. The next time you attend a party where you *do* know the people, think about that poor girl over in the corner who is alone and trying desperately to look as if she isn't. What can you do to make her feel less lonely?

Whatever makes you lonely undoubtedly makes someone else lonely, too. Your girlfriend may be lonely some evening and unendingly grateful for a telephone call or an invitation to come over and watch TV or sew. Use the alone times to heighten your sensitivity to the loneliness of others.

Do You Really Like Yourself?

The more mature we become the better use we are able to make of our moments alone. The essence of healthy aloneness, of course, is self-love—not in any selfish sense, but in the sense of: Do you like yourself? Do you feel comfortable with yourself? Can you entertain yourself, keep yourself company, or does someone else have to entertain you? Are you your own best friend? If you don't like yourself, it stands to reason you won't enjoy being alone with yourself.

The second greatest commandment given by Jesus was to love your neighbor *as you love yourself* (*see* Matthew 22:39). In his *Commentary on the Whole Bible,* Matthew Henry tells us, "There is a self-love which is corrupt, and the root of the greatest sins, and it must be put off and mortified: but there is a self-love which is natural, and the rule of the greatest duty, and it must be preserved and sanctified. We must love ourselves, that is, we must have a due regard to the dignity of our own natures, and a due concern for the welfare of our own souls and bodies."

You cannot be a true friend to someone else unless you are on friendly terms with yourself. You cannot accept someone else until you accept yourself. You cannot truly love someone else until you first love God and then yourself.

Additional Tips for Handling Loneliness

From *Getting Started* by Gary R. Collins

Loneliness is a common experience, especially during the early adult years when there is change, mobility, and sometimes insecurity in relating to others. The following suggestions can be helpful.

1. Admit that you struggle with loneliness.
2. Ponder the possible causes of your loneliness.
3. Consider what you could do to change.
4. Look for opportunities to be with people.
5. Resist self-pity.
6. Ask God to meet your loneliness needs.
7. Accept the fact that some things will not change.

Some women prefer having a roommate to living by themselves. Sometimes it works, sometimes it doesn't. When the benefits outweigh the frustrations you will usually find two (or more) people interested in helping each other grow by using the special tools called the three C's:

Compromise is first, because roommates who always want their own way don't stay roommates very long.

Communication is an overused word, but an underdeveloped skill with most of us.

Confrontation is the most delicate tool of all. We shy away from it but it aids tremendously in overcoming relationship barriers. It's a tough area for personal growth. You have to take a hard look at confrontations and why you dislike them. You have to see yourself as other people see you, particularly when you shy away from a confrontation experience. You have to come to grips with making significant changes in your life.

2

Living with Your Family of Friends

From *Today's Christian Woman* Magazine
Spring 1983
by Susan Luckey

Somewhere between fleeing the nest and building your own, singles often experience living with roommates—a rewarding, if stretching, fact of life. From the first dorm room shared with a stranger to an apartment with a special friend, to a house full of people thrown together out of necessity, sharing living quarters engages you in the process known as chipping off the rough edges.

Most of us long for "our own place," where we have total freedom over where to hang each picture and when to take out the trash. But the high cost of living alone and the isolation that occurs in a busy world motivate many of us to find a roommate and set up housekeeping. Yet, even if we know and love the person we choose to live with, we soon realize that no two people do the same thing the same way. With the fun and close times come inevitable conflicts that test the very foundation of a friendship.

In some ways a roommate situation is similar to a marriage, though without many of its benefits or its security. A roommate sees us in the morning before we've brushed out teeth or put on our makeup. She sees us grumpy, silly, selfish, unattractive. A husband will also see us that way, but he's made a commitment to love us nevertheless; a roommate often has not. A husband has committed himself to stay with us forever. A roommate may choose to leave at anytime, even after a deep relationship has developed. I've heard people say that being a roommate prepares you for marriage. But, whether you eventually get married or not, living with another provides an excellent education in the give-and-take of life.

There are several ways to approach life with roommates. Some believe in the hit-and-run option. You live together but go your own ways, rarely taking time to get to know each other. A roommate is just someone to help pay the rent.

Another approach I call "camping out." You live in the same place but no one really takes much responsibility around the house. And you don't work too hard at building deep relationships. After all, it's only temporary.

Others like a living situation that resembles a family. They believe they're together for a reason, that God is using qualities in each person to build up the other. This kind of household may be highly structured or more loosely defined, but the feeling is the same—you're committed to another person's growth. There's a willingness to get below the surface and share each other's needs—to be available and vulnerable.

Though the latter living style involves some risks (being genuine with another person and giving up some of our personal territory can be scary), the benefits are many. They include a flexibility that is only learned through: not always getting our own way; seeing ourselves through the eyes of another—and facing what we see there; and learning how to confront people without destroying a relationship and without having to call someone up in the middle of the night when we need somebody to talk to. I call these benefits the three C's of getting along with people, especially roommates: compromise, communication and confrontation.

Compromise. Of course, we all know that our way is the best, but there are times when not everybody sees it that way. I like a tidy house. Invariably I have at least one roommate who leaves a trail of socks, cellophane wrappers, and empty soda cans wherever she goes. Another roomie swept the floor industriously, only to leave the pile of dirt in the corner.

I tried to teach by example, but got irritated when my roomies didn't pick up the clues. If I vacuumed six times in a row, everyone would appreciate my effort but not volunteer to do it the next time. My attitude was not that of a servant but of a judge. When I decided to let my roommates be themselves, I experienced a real peace. I could vacuum without ulterior motives and go my way without holding a grudge. When I began to tend to the log in my own eye instead of the speck in my roommates', I saw positive change in their habits. And doubtless my roommates enjoyed being around me much more when I wasn't pestering them to do this or that.

Sometimes compromise may even mean staying up watching TV (when I'd rather sequester myself in my room with a good book), just to spend some time with my roommate.

Communication. Once an incoming roommate replaced a roommate who had become my best friend. I wasn't ready to open myself up to someone new, so I went my own way, neither shutting out my new roommate nor taking her into my confidence. But she wanted to get to know me. Despite a busy schedule, she made it a point to be available when I got home from work—to talk or to just be there. I usually carried about a half hour's worth of frazzledness home from the office and wasn't always interested in being around anyone when I first walked through the door. But her consistent attention worked. In a few months I considered her one of my closest friends, and it certainly wasn't my doing. When she told me what she'd done to win my friendship, I was amazed. It had never occurred to me *not* to let a friendship "just happen."

Communication takes work. It means giving up our comfortable silence to extend ourselves to another person. In a living situation, it means keeping the lines open. If you've had a bad day, simply saying, "I feel rotten, so don't take it personally, but I feel like I need some room right now," may ease another's worry and guilt. Or being transparent enough to say, "I'm feeling lonesome and I really need some attention right now," may be a revolutionary step for some of us.

You may be saying to yourself, "Well, that's fine if your roommates are sensitive and trustworthy; but I don't know if I can risk myself that way." You may be right. But I have found that love breeds love, trust breeds trust. If I don't give someone a chance to respond to me in a loving way, I may never know the compassion hidden in that person. If I wait until they confide in me before I divulge my own hopes and fears . . . well, the opportunity may never come to let down the barriers. This leads directly to the third C.

Confrontation. Oh, what an awful word! For some of us, conflict of any kind is negative, something to be avoided at all costs. Others of us have an unreined temper and leave a path of destruction wherever we go. But confrontation can be constructive.

Many problems that lead to unpleasant confrontations can be alleviated by "house meetings," where complaints are aired in a controlled atmosphere. It's important, however, not to turn these meetings into a time of discussing each other's worst faults. Diplomacy and sensitivity are the keys. Avoid openers such as, "Tell me what you think is my worst fault and I'll tell you what I think is yours and we'll each promise to take it like adults." Though tempting, the resulting discussion may irreparably damage a friendship.

Sooner or later, in almost any relationship, problems arise that won't disappear simply by being ignored. Jesus advised us not to let the sun go down on our anger because festering wounds are a playground for the enemy. Somewhere in between holding hurts in so tightly they have to be pried out and blurting out the first comment that comes to our minds, lies the kind of honest, open communication about grievances we're looking for. Even so, confrontations can be complicated when one or both parties gets defensive. Be prepared to go through some unpleasantries to work out a problem.

Of course, sometimes so many problems have piled up that pressure needs to be applied to ease the tension. I have learned never to confront anyone, however, before I've spent time praying and asking the Lord to work in both of our hearts. Jumping in too fast may do more harm than good. Once you're convinced of the need for a confrontation, choose an appropriate time and start a discussion in a way that isn't accusatory. Phrases like, "Have I done something to upset you? . . . Can we talk about it?" may serve to get a talk started. If a person is intent on harboring ill feelings, I may have to pursue her into the other room and say something like, "I'm not leaving until you tell me what's wrong." Or, "I know something is bothering you and I need you to tell me about it because the tension in this house is driving me crazy." Sound undignified? Possibly. But it may take some digging to get a person who is torturing herself with unspoken anger to open up.

One of my roommates hated to communicate her feelings. She

felt that Christians could only express good feelings, so she dammed up the bad ones to the point that our whole household held our collective breaths and exchanged helpless glances when she walked into the room. Finally, I couldn't take the tension anymore and in a fairly awkward way forced the storm cloud to explode. It took some downright graceless communication, raised voices and all, to get the anger out. We ended in tears and hugged each other. Though raw from painful feelings that had finally been spoken, we were happier and more at ease than we'd been in weeks. That exchange was a turning point for her in learning not to bottle up her feelings and for me in seeing the good side of confronting negative situations head-on.

One rule my roommates and I have tried to live by is: don't leave the argument until we've come to a meeting of the hearts. It's easy to unload on a victim and stomp out of the room. It is much more difficult to unload and then deal with the consequences of what we've said, and to give the other person the same opportunity. It's hard to admit our mistakes, to cry together, and to finally carry the whole works to the Father in prayer. But the rewards of that kind of confrontation are great. My most precious friends are those whom I have hurt or who have hurt me, who paid the price of working out those tender feelings, forgiving and loving through the ordeal. We've seen each other without angelic masks and we still care.

Perhaps we'll be fortunate enough to live with people who are well-adjusted, who know how to communicate honestly and openly, who have mastered the art of affirmation and edification, who are selfless and wise. And maybe we'll even act that way ourselves. Many of us, like me, will have to climb, and occasionally climb again, the mountains of compromise, communication, and confrontation. But when I think of warm, cozy afternoons spent in spontaneous coffee klatches with friends around our rickety kitchen table, I know it's worth the struggle.

What holds a one-parent family together? Is it even possible to function as a family when you wind up divorced or widowed? Maybe the first thing you will have to do is convince your mother to stop calling your kids "those poor little half orphans." Here are some tips by a very wise lady who has spent many years as a single parent.

3

Single Parents: Keeping Your Family Intact

From *Today's Christian Woman* Magazine
Winter 1980–81
by Elizabeth Hormann

Is there family life after a marriage breaks up or a spouse dies? Many women are finding that a broken marriage or death of a mate, no matter how devastating, need not result in a broken home. Renewing a sense of family after one parent is gone can be difficult but not impossible. Here are some ways one parent found to put her family back together again.

1. Create a wholesome atmosphere. When my marriage ended, I sensed that the quality of our family life was going to be determined in some ways by the attitudes of the people around us. I made it clear from the start that ours was not a broken home, that I was not a swinging single with five short roommates. We were a family, sharing a very difficult experience, but a real family, nonetheless.

Because the year before the separation had been so stressful, I expected the children would be more relaxed once they got used to the situation. I told their teachers to look for some positive changes. Not surprisingly, they found what I told them they were looking for. I discouraged my mother from calling them "those poor little half orphans," introduced the children to other single parent families, and planned a few special events for the first summer to give some substance to my pep talk about a better life.

But I didn't overdo it. Too much pep talk can develop into the divorce-as-a-wonderful-opportunity-for-personal-growth approach and I don't really see divorce that way. I was hurt and angry that my marriage didn't last; my children were hurt and angry, too, and they needed to vent those feelings. In the early months, we cried as much as we laughed; shouted in anger as much as in joy and had three Earnest Discussions for every frivolous one. We continued to be a family, but we had to work out new ways of living together, and that was serious business.

2. *Maintain order.* In many two-parent homes, each adult takes over areas traditionally labeled as "his" or "hers," and the children are assigned jobs more because it is good for them than because they are needed. But in the single parent family, the children really are needed. This does not mean that the single parent should share the authority in the household with one of her children.

My children, already used to helping around the house, were told just how important they were to the smooth running of our home. They knew it was to their advantage to cooperate (if only to avoid a grouchy mother), but they also knew I could manage alone if I had to and that I stood between them and any real disaster.

3. *Schedule "unscheduled" time.* I try to plan for other family needs as well by leaving blocks of time unscheduled for talking, playing a game, reading a story, or other spur-of-the-moment things that make family life a pleasure. Scheduling free time allows me to feel that I am supposed to be relaxing and ensures that I don't cheat my family with obsessive working.

4. *Extend your family.* Single parent families do not thrive well in solitude. They need connections with other people to feel part of a larger family and the community. The ties to extended family are especially important in helping single parents and their children feel they are "normal" and part of a "real" family.

Before they died, my parents lived nearby. My father, crippled by arthritis, was an ideal grandfather, attuned to the pace of small children. My mother happily took the children bargain hunting at flea markets, passed along to them her librarian's respect for good books, and shared their taste in movies more readily than I can.

We are a little short in the aunt and uncle department, but I have scores of relatives of the second cousin (or first cousin twice removed, depending) variety. Many of them I have come to know only in adulthood, but my children are meeting them early in life, forming strong bonds, and learning that the degree of kinship depends more on emotional ties than blood ties.

Close friends are another sort of extended family. We made some very good friends at the single parent camp our church runs each year. If the warmth and caring of Christian friends is important to me, it is probably even more important that my children grow up with the companionship and leadership of other people who are committed to Christ.

5. Work at making memories. Because single parent families often have some very unhappy experiences in their backgrounds, it is important to create happy times together. I've been fortunate to have work that requires some traveling. When the children were small I took them all with me. As they grew older, I took only a couple at a time (rotating them to be fair) and gave them a chance to concentrate on just one sibling for a few days.

Because my ancestors were not only prolific but nomads as well, we have family spread all over the country. Every trip becomes a family reunion, and when we stay home, the family comes to visit. The ties become stronger every year ... and we are happier for them.

Seventeen years ago, when I first became a parent, I envisioned family life quite differently from the way it turned out. By the time my last child is grown, I will have spent eighty percent of my parenting years as a single parent. It is often difficult, but then it isn't always easy for two-parent families, either. It's only as they work around the troubles and take pleasure in the good times that any group of people stays intact and becomes a real family.

Part Two

---◆---

Learn Your Music: In Tune With Our Life-Style

A career is very important in the life of a so-loing woman. Can a woman be as successful as a man in the business world? How can she get where she wants to be? The first thing she needs is patience. Don't lose heart when the objective you anticipate reaching is not always attained. Remember, we are dealing with reality, not perfection. Mastery of any career takes lots of practice and with practice you *will improve*. To succeed as a woman in business takes more than just trying. It takes continual cognizance, evaluation, sensitivity, and a willingness to switch gears when necessary. It also takes one other quality that every woman already has and all men lack. It's our secret weapon. Never neglect it to be "one of the boys."

4

What in the World Are You Doing?

From *Single* by Marilyn McGinnis

Margo's enjoyment of her nursing career was obvious. Always happy and cheerful with her patients, she had many opportunities to share Christ.

When I met Janet she was an elevator operator and embarrassed about it. "She doesn't want anyone to know what she does," a friend confided.

Why was one girl happy in her job and another not? Is there something wrong with being an elevator operator? Of course not. The key lies in each girl's attitude toward her work.

The single years offer unlimited opportunities to pursue meaningful work goals. You are free to travel when and where you wish. With a little scrimping here and there you can get as much schooling as you need or want. You can choose the kind of work you most enjoy with less thought about salary and location because you don't have to help support five children or pay off a thirty-year mortgage on the house. You are free as a bird (within the bounds of God's will for your life) to choose a profession that interests you and advance in it.

Why, then, are there Janets in this world who don't like their jobs and make sure other people know it?

Some women have one-track minds which hinder their enjoyment of anything else. They want to get married. Period. Nothing but marriage interests them. A job is a necessary evil to keep from starving to death until a husband comes along. All their thoughts and energies are channeled toward dreaming about the day when they will marry.

"Just the other day I was asked what my ambition in life was," writes a twenty-six-year-old woman. "This started me thinking, and I answered quite bluntly that it was to get married, settle down, and raise a family. I've never felt settled in anything that I've done yet. I'm one confused kid and have always felt that I'm just filling in time and space, and that someday I'd find what I was looking for if I kept trying different things.

"Don't mistake me," she continues, "I am waiting for the Lord to lead. I'm not going to jump into marriage until I find the right one. But no men are in sight yet so I must continue to fill in time and space."

If God wants you to marry, then marriage for you is a worthy goal. But not if it causes you to lose interest in everything else in life. Involvement in a meaningful occupation prior to marriage can help prepare you to be a good mate. Through your job you can learn new skills, gain new knowledge, meet new and interesting people, and share your faith with others. Suppose you do marry and suddenly find yourself widowed or divorced. Many a woman has wished she had job training and experience to fall back on when she suddenly finds herself the sole support of the family. The woman with the one-track mind for marriage misses out on the important things a good job can contribute to her life. Buried in those ever-present dreams of matrimony she may even miss out on some very important dates. No man is impressed with a woman whose only topic of conversation is matrimony. In fact it will probably frighten him away!

Let's face it. A job is also a status symbol. A married woman's status is determined largely by who she's married to. A single woman's status is determined by what she does for a living.

There are many reasons a woman may be dissatisfied with her job, and some of them are perfectly legitimate. Perhaps you have taken a job for which you are underqualified (causing frustration) or overqualified (causing boredom). If so, take the additional training needed to become qualified or look around for something more challenging. The important thing is to *enjoy* what you are doing.

Your attitude toward your work tells a lot about you as a person.

If you enjoy your work, your happiness will radiate to others. If you dislike your work, your negative attitude will spread like wildfire. First you hate your job. Then you begin to dislike the people with whom you work. Pretty soon you become sarcastic, critical, and perhaps even downright rude. And eventually your attitude will spread to your friends.

"If you are miserable or bored in your work," says Bruce Larson in his book *Dare to Live Now,* "or dread going to it, then God is speaking to you. He either wants to change the job you are in— or—more likely—He wants to change *you.*"

If you are unhappy with your job, ask yourself a few questions.

1. *Is the work interesting and challenging?* Do you look forward to going to work in the morning (well, *most* mornings, anyway)? Or do the eight hours at work seem like an eternity?

   If boredom is the theme, chances are you are capable of much more than the job offers. Are there other jobs in the company that would be more interesting? Why not apply for them? Or perhaps you'd rather be in a different line of work altogether. Find out what kind of training is necessary and go after it. Thirty-five or forty hours a week is a lot of time to spend doing something you hate. If sheer laziness is your only excuse for not pursuing more interesting work, shame on you!

2. *Is the salary adequate?* If salary is your only consideration in looking for a job, you'll be in big trouble. At the same time, however, the Bible says the workman is worthy of his hire. There is no reason you should settle for a mediocre salary if the same job at a better salary is available.

   My first year and a half out of college I worked as secretary to the department head of a Christian institution. My salary was pitifully low. Even with minimal expenses I went in the hole financially every month. I appealed to my boss and to his boss for a raise in pay but neither was able to give it to me. I was perfectly willing to live "on faith," but the seriousness of my financial condition finally convinced me that that was not the kind of faith God wanted me to live on. I quit my job and got a secretarial position with a company that paid a substantially higher salary. Because of the increased income I was able to save enough money to allow me to tackle graduate school a year and a half later.

3. *Does the work you are doing dishonor Christ in any way?* Is your company laced with shady dealings? There are few companies in this world that are 100 percent honest. But for the most part, a company is either on the up-and-up or it isn't. Are you ever asked to juggle the books, lie to customers, or pad reports with misinformation? If so, it is not likely God would want you to remain in such an organization.

4. *Are you in God's will to the best of your ability?* Margo's love for her work and her Christian testimony to her patients was obvious evidence that she was in God's will. Janet's attitude toward her job as an elevator operator, however, indicated something was wrong. Perhaps it was a matter of pride, a feeling that "I'm too good for this kind of job." In that case maybe God was trying to teach her something about humility. Perhaps she was just too lazy to take whatever training was necessary to find a more enjoyable job. It is also possible that she had simply never accepted the fact that this was the place in which God wanted her to serve Him. A cheerful elevator operator who radiates the love of Christ can have a tremendous influence on the people she serves, especially in an office building where she meets the same people day after day. But to have that kind of ministry she must willingly accept the fact that this is God's place of service for her—at least until He shows her something else. The cheerfulness that makes her a good operator may also help her move up the ladder when a more challenging job becomes available.

If you are unhappy with your job or are simply filling in time at a job until Mr. Right comes along, take a good long look at yourself. Either you or your job needs to change.

Let's assume now that you've found a job you really like. Just what does it take to be successful on the job and move up the company ladder?

Someone has suggested that to be successful in business a woman must be able to look like a woman, act like a lady, and think like a man! And there's a great deal of truth in that simple statement. The way in which a woman conducts herself in the business world is vitally important to her Christian testimony and her role as a woman.

Look Like a Woman

An important part of looking like a woman is just that—looking like a *woman*. Today's casual styles often make it difficult to tell the boys from the girls. Leave your blue jeans at home. Businesslike suits and dresses are much more appropriate and always in style.

Dress as attractively as your budget will permit and keep your hair well groomed (clean and shiny!) in the style most becoming to you. Slim down if you're overweight. Fatten up if you're too thin. Take a good look in a full-length mirror every morning before you leave for the office. Be neat, clean, and as attractive as possible. With the variety of hair styles, makeup specialists, and fashion consultants available today, no woman has any excuse for not looking her very best.

Act Like a Lady

Avoid extremes in clothing styles—short, short skirts, low necklines, layers and layers of ruffles. Conservative is best for the office.

Be careful about office romances. Some organizations prohibit fraternization between employees. If this is the policy where you work, abide by it. And even if it isn't a policy, be careful. If you date a fellow employee and things don't work out, going to work can be pretty grim.

Contrary to popular opinion, it is not necessary to have an affair with your boss in order to get ahead. If it *is* necessary in your company, the job isn't worth it.

Another area where a Christian woman has to be careful is in the area of "business dates"—having lunch or dinner with your boss or other married men in the company. A situation that once, no doubt, caused raised eyebrows is now quite commonplace and not necessarily bad. It all depends on the reason for such business dates.

Many business dates are a necessary part of the business world and need not be refused. Sometimes lunch or dinner is the only time left in a busy day to talk about important business. In such cases this is part of your job. However, do what you can to avoid dark, intimate restaurants or other questionable situations which might cause talk. You have as much responsibility to protect your boss's reputation as to protect your own.

Think Like a Man

This, of course, is impossible and no man really wants you to. But you can and must be businesslike and professional like a man. When things go wrong, avoid emotional outbursts (anger or tears) which are quickly labeled "just like a woman." Men view the business world objectively, logically, and without emotion.

Keep your personal problems out of the office as much as possible. If you need to confide in someone, go to your minister or a close friend outside the office.

Be honest. Don't take pencils or paper clips or cheat on your time card. You may think you're getting away with something, but eventually dishonesty takes its toll.

Despite some of the commendable efforts of women's libbers, it is still possible you may not make as much money as a man in a position similar to yours. And you may not receive as many promotions as he does, either. It just may be that your attitude is what's holding you back from a promotion, not the fact that you are a woman. If your company is hard-nosed about promoting women, move on to a company where you will have more freedom.

Don't talk too much. This includes gossiping, which is a deadly pastime. Remember Thumper, the rabbit? He always used to say, "If you can't say something good about somebody, don't say nuthin' at all." It also includes general office chitchat which is unnecessary and distracting. Coffee breaks and lunch hours are for socializing. In between, keep unnecessary talk to a minimum.

Keep company secrets. If your boss tells you something in confidence, don't open your mouth. And don't discuss your company's shortcomings outside the company. If you don't like the company, go somewhere else. Don't take out your frustrations by unloading its faults on others. Loyalty is an important commodity on the path to success.

Okay, suppose for ten years you were married and during that time you were not gainfully employed. Then, through a chain of unpleasant or tragic events, you found yourself divorced or widowed. You were suddenly without a mate and forced to enter the workaday world again. That could be a frightening experience. *Good grief,* you'd think, *I've lost all my marketable skills. I'm too old, too discouraged, too behind the times. The areas in which I excelled are now all run by computers. What am I going to do?* Does that sound like a rerun of your jumbled thoughts when you lie awake at night worrying about all of the problems you will have to face once you put your feet on the floor? Cheer up! This next chapter is just for you.

Ch.

5

New Career Beginnings

From *Suddenly Single* by Jim Smoke

Newly divorced and fifty-three years old, she stopped by my office on her way home from the employment agency. Amid a sea of tears and a deeply crushed spirit, she told me of her two-hour ordeal trying to find a job. After she had answered many questions and filled out a blizzard of paperwork, the counselor informed her that she had no marketable skills and would probably have to go back to school in order to obtain some training for the job openings available.

In the time I have spent working with newly single people, I have listened to this story hundreds of times. The only variable is the age of the applicant. The response is usually the same. The reality is that the world is not waiting to hire women who are suddenly single again through the death or divorce of a mate.

A vast number of women affected by divorce must find a way to survive economically in an already overloaded job market. Many of them have been out of the work force for twenty to thirty years. The fact that you worked in a library when you were twenty-two has little bearing on job economics in the eighties. Many women dust off a twenty-year-old degree in sociology or English, only to find out that today's more skilled graduates form a long line in front of them. It is easy for the lines of discouragement to form a circle around your worst fears.

A number of people I have met have switched from the employment line to the welfare line. Their despair at losing a mate is compounded by their despair at not finding meaningful employment.

Beginning again in the working world is no easy task. The few who have worked during their marriages are least affected. They simply continue on. The others often end up with meaningless and mundane jobs simply to have a few dollars coming in. Still others are convinced they will never find a decent job, and their pursuit switches to finding someone who will support them so that they will not have to work.

Becoming single again at any age means many new beginnings in your life. Few things stay as they once were. Some of those changes can be welcome adventures in new growth. One such area is your career.

Keeping On

Many people already have very satisfying jobs when they find themselves suddenly single again. The job may be so satisfying that they try to hide in it during their period of loss. Their former eight-hour day becomes a sixteen-hour day with overtime on weekends included. They feel that drowning themselves in their work will keep the pain away. While men may be more inclined to deal with their emotional upsets this way, women might do the same thing.

Work can become an obsession. It can also seem to be the only area in which you have any control over your life. A lack of achievement in family life and marriage can mean a frantic rush to gain some measurable success in your job.

On the other hand, keeping on in your present work can be a good form of therapy. It can take your mind off some of the problems that cannot be solved today. It can fill potentially empty time, and create a sense of fulfillment and self-worth.

Changing

When many things are changing around you, some by choice and some by chance, it gives you the opportunity for a total reevaluation of every area in your life. One of the areas that many people look at last is the career area. Somehow, you feel that this area is too sacred to tamper with or evaluate. Or your fear of making changes drives you back to the security of leaving things as they are. One of the positive things that comes with becoming single again is the opportunity to take a long look at your job, career, or vocation, and ask yourself the question "Is this really what I want to do?" I will admit, this is a risky question for everyone, single or married.

Several years ago, I asked that question myself. The answer produced some profound changes in my own life that moved me from the security of a church ministry to a national traveling and speaking ministry. I also discovered that you will run into two types of people when you make this kind of drastic change in your life.

The first type of person questions your change and tells you that he or she would not have done it if they had the choice. They dredge up a long list of fears, and finally tell you that they simply can't understand how you could do that kind of thing. They are the discouragers!

The second type of person is the one who, when told of your change, tells you how excited he is for you and affirms your decision in every way. He is an encourager! We all need lots of this variety in our lives, and as few as possible of the first variety. Too many people, while reevaluating a career decision, go from person to person in a "pooling of ignorance" routine. They ask everyone's opinion and either do nothing or do what the last person they were with told them to do.

Sound and trusted counsel and input is always valuable, while a collection of opinions just confuses the issue. There are several questions I have used numerous times in my life when I am faced with evaluating changes. Get a pencil and answer these for yourself. It could mean the beginning of some changes in your career.

Why are you doing what you are now doing? Sometimes when I travel, I use this question in getting to know the people who pick me up at the airport. I usually ask them first what they do in their job. They respond easily to that. When I follow it with a "Why do you do that?" question, I sometimes get a confused look. Some respond by saying, "I've always done that." Others tell me that they were trained for that specific job years ago. Still others tell me that their family has been doing that certain job for over a hundred years.

I am sure that all of these responses are very legitimate. I am not sure that they are always valid. Many people today are leaving jobs and careers that they were trained for, and are starting over. Sometimes the challenge is gone and the career becomes a sentence that will be relieved only by death. I meet many people who are extremely unhappy with their jobs. I wonder why they continue to do them. Fear of change? Fear of what others will think? Fear of failure? Fear of financial loss? Fear of success? Probably a little of each.

Some people get into jobs temporarily, until something else comes along. Nothing new comes crashing through the door, and they simply settle into a rut after a time. They can wake up ten years later with a locked-in feeling, wondering how they got there in the first place. If you take a job temporarily, keep reminding yourself of that. That job is simply a passageway to the next part of your journey.

Are you happy and fulfilled in what you are doing? We spend many hours during a lifetime at our employment. If our work is exciting, rewarding, and challenging, we will be fulfilled. If it is a dull and weary experience, we will have a lot of misery. That misery will carry over into every other area of our lives. It will affect our families, children, relationships, and our own physical and mental health.

Happiness in a job is being happy while you are doing it and being happy with the results that come out of your job. It is doing the job well and meeting new challenges as you do it. When the challenge goes out of a job, boredom sets in. Weekends and holidays become release and relief from the job. What is that about your job that makes you happy right now? Take your pencil and continue the list.

Is your present job the best investment of your abilities and talents? Each of us brings to any task in life a vast assortment of the abilities we possess. Some of those tasks call forth a wide variety of what we have. Others need very little. Unused abilities and talents get rusty and decay. Only the talents we call up to use stay sharp and honed. As they are used increasingly, they become perfected. When was the last time you listed all of your abilities and talents? Have you had your close friends confirm those things you see in yourself as well as what they see in you?

One of the best ways to identify your own gifts is to have others call them out of you. It is the little-league coach who watches a new player swing the bat with confidence and natural ease. He sees in him the power to be a hitter. He views him on a major-league team down the road. His job is to call that gift out and affirm it. Some people are doing jobs and are locked in careers that either misuse their abilities or don't use them at all. Your personal satisfaction and happiness will be at stake if you are in a position that does not use your abilities to their fullest.

The world has a lot of people in the wrong places. The key is that you don't have to stay in the wrong place. You can move and change and make steps toward where you want to be. Take your pencil out again and list your gifts, talents, and abilities. Are you using them in your present job or career?

What would you rather do right now than what you are doing? If I left a blank space right here, I think I know the first thing many of you would write. Retire! Go to Hawaii or the South Seas to live! Never work again!

I lived in Florida for a number of years, and I used to watch the endless migration of retirees who finally accumulated enough years at their occupations to get the gold watch and retire to a neat mobile-home park in the sun. For the first months, they bragged that this really was the way to go. After the initial excitement wore off, they started looking around for something meaningful to do with their time. Few seemed to find it. Many started drinking as a release from their boredom.

Some things appear to be what we want, until we get them in our grasp. It's like the child who wants many new toys and gifts for Christmas, and ends the day playing with the empty boxes they came in. Asking the above question is not intended to send you on a flight into fantasy. It is to help you look at other viable options for your life. Some people have dropped their lifelong careers and turned their satisfying hobbies into jobs. If you get more satisfaction and fulfillment from your hobby than your career, perhaps you should think about this kind of change.

Martha is a good example of a single-again person who made a hobby-to-career change. Her hobby was refurbishing old houses that were run down and unsalable. She started buying these little ramshackle places that nobody wanted. In a few short months, with her deft decorating skills, the houses were transformed and sold, often on the first day of their listing.

Martha slowly moved along with buying, renovating, and reselling until before long her hobby employed many others who worked along with her. She often had four or five houses under repair at the same time. Soon she was buying larger and more expensive homes and giving them the same treatment. When I last spoke to her, she had built a whole empire in the real-estate world and had hired a property manager to keep track of all her holdings. Martha had made the giant leap from a fun hobby to a prosperous career.

I have had some single-again people tell me that their job or career is their joy in life and they would rather do that than anything else. That's usually a good test of the above question. If you would rather do nothing else than what you are currently doing, you are probably being fulfilled in your present situation—either that or you are making too much money to change to what you really want to do. Take a minute and list your "rathers." Are some of them feasible for you? What would it take to accomplish them? Do you find yourself getting excited at the possibilities?

What did you want to do when you were a child? Most parents ask their children what they want to be when they grow up. If they want to be in a prestigious profession, the parents then brag to everyone within earshot that their Johnny or Mary is going to be a doctor, lawyer, and so forth, when they grow up. Some children grow up with their precast careers taking shape around them. To follow any other would be a grave disappointment to their parents and fellowman.

Many little boys who won speech contests in school were told by their parents that they would be great preachers someday. Thirty years later, they found themselves in a career that they were ill equipped to handle in areas other than speech. Childhood is a time to dream great dreams of tomorrow. For some of us, those dreams become obstacles that prevent us from doing what we really want to do. For others, the dreams were forgotten for more realistic pursuits. I am not so sure that the things we showed great interest in as children should have passed away as we matured.

Being single again can be a time to think through some of those dreams and perhaps begin their pursuit. It was not until my father's death that my mother was able to pursue her childhood dream of becoming a nurse. For a number of years prior to her death, she was able to do something she had always wanted to do. Many children abandon their dreams because they are told by ill-informed parents that they are too stupid, too small, too unathletic, too poor in math, and so on. Many newly divorced people have told me that they had been convinced by their spouses over the years that they could not do certain things, only to find out after the divorce that this was untrue. Many of us will never grow up. We will be changing, growing, trying, and thinking new things throughout life.

Starting Over

Moving ahead and making changes accounts for a certain segment of the newly single-again population. These are people who are in jobs and careers or who are changing from one thing they have been doing to another they desire. What about the mother with three children and fourteen years of housewifing to her credit? With the death or divorce of a mate, the economic situation in one's life changes rapidly. In many homes, the mother has to seek employment. With few up-to-date skills, where does she go and what does she do?

Most major colleges and universities across America have added women's departments to their programs. One such program in our area is called "Reentry Options for Women." It deals with bringing a nonworking woman into the work force. It is not an employment agency. It goes well beyond that, as it attempts to interview, test, and educate women to what is available.

The job market of twenty years ago is vastly different from that of today. Many jobs that existed then are obsolete today. Even your college major may be obsolete. New jobs and career opportunities are being born every day. Many are looking for people. Most people don't know they exist.

The old myth that a woman must take a "servant" position or job is long gone. Women, in recent years, have obtained positions in the executive world once dominated by men. The accomplishments of the women's movement in the seventies will update many single women on the progress that has been made.

Educational opportunities abound. The listing of evening adult-education classes offered by the colleges in my own area is incredible. Training is available for every conceivable career or job. Classes are held at convenient hours. Many are free while others have reasonable charges. Perhaps the greatest fear a woman has in looking into a new career or even a first career is that her choice will be wrong. Don't let that deter you. You have the freedom to test the waters and move on to another situation if you choose to. There is nothing that says you have to be stuck in one career just because you started it. That kind of thinking becomes a trap to growth.

Another thing to be wary of is being sold on a certain field of employment because there are numerous openings or because the field offers great security. Neither of these aspects will mean much to you if you are unhappy with what you are doing. You need to do your own homework and make sure that you want to try a certain area. Don't let others talk you into something you really don't want to do.

Have you done your homework yet? Drop by your local college or university. Check out what it has to offer. Take the testing program. Sign up for a course or two. Investigate all the opportunities. Let yourself get excited!

Waiting to Be Rescued

A little earlier in the chapter, I mentioned a group of people who look around for someone to support them so they won't have to face some of the things I have talked about. Waiting to be rescued from singleness is deadly. First, you will never know whether you had what it takes to be responsible for your own life. Second, your knight in white may deliver you from employment and its frustrations but bring far more hazardous problems into your life.

Many single-again people are willing to make a trade-off in this area. I am never quite sure that they understand what they can lose. I cannot stress enough the feelings of self-confidence, self-worth, and self-accomplishment that come from the new beginnings of career development.

Too Old and Tired?

I frequently speak with single-again people who are over sixty. When they hear me talking about new jobs and developing new interests, they sigh and tell me that they are too old and too tired to attempt anything. I am always amazed because as I read the Bible I find that God really doesn't seem to care much about age. Retirement is not mentioned in the Scriptures. Moses was well into his eighties when he undertook his greatest leadership assignment.

In today's world, Colonel Sanders and Grandma Moses were apparently late bloomers. Their success came well after age sixty-five. Many older singles seem content to serve time. Their unhappiness and lethargy is largely due to their lack of motivation and belief in themselves. Age has nothing to do with growth. New opportunities come to open minds and open hearts.

New Road Ahead

If you are past the crisis of losing a mate by death or divorce, it's time to start looking at your future. It is in your hands. Don't get locked in a holding pattern. Spend some time alone asking yourself some hard questions about your vocational tomorrows. Get with some trusted resource people and let them help you. Start planning for yourself. Take some of the little steps that will get you going. Celebrate your progress! You are on a new road!

Different from *starting over*, but in some ways more difficult, is the challenge of *starting out*. If you are a struggling soloist, feeling all alone out there, don't go any further without learning two valuable secrets. First, be patient with yourself, then, of equal importance, defer your rewards. Set your goals, plan well in advance, and learn to think of the future while working in the present to earn your basic credentials. All this takes practice and sacrifice, but the benefits of deferred gratification make the toils and encumbrances of the present worth the wait.

6

Becoming a Career Builder

From *Getting Started* by Gary R. Collins

Getting established in a career is one of the biggest challenges of the young adult years. It is a challenge fraught with excitement and frustration, success and disappointing failures. It is a task that might be helped if you remember several basic truisms.

First, life is not easy. M. Scott Peck called this "a great truth, one of the greatest truths," but most of us don't believe it, at least until we reach middle age. Instead, we complain about problems, try to avoid them or find someone else to solve them, and live with the assumption that life should be easy—as it so often is on television. Such an attitude fails to recognize that, as Peck says in *The Road Less Traveled,* "it is in the whole process of meeting and solving problems that life has its meaning. . . . It is only because of problems that we grow mentally and spiritually."

Second, it helps to remember that life isn't always fair. Most of us would like to believe otherwise, but as we grow older we realize that some people get ahead through dishonesty, that hard work doesn't always pay off in this world, and that *who you know* is sometimes more important than *what you know.* Armed with these facts, we are not free to be dishonest or sloppy in our work, but a lot of frustration can be avoided if we recognize that there is injustice on this planet, and that sometimes you and I are its victims. It also can be helpful to read Psalm 73 periodically.

Third, realize that there is limited room at the top. This has always been true, but in recent years, the baby-boom population has swelled both the labor force and the numbers of people competing for a few places of leadership in the business and professional worlds. A generation that grew up expecting success and the good life is finding that only a few "make it." The philosophy of certain success through positive mental attitude is leaving thousands frustrated when confronted with the hard realities of life.

Fourth, would you agree that everybody can be successful? Much depends on how we define *success.* In our society, power, prestige, and possessions are the major marks of success, and the life goals for a lot of people. But for many of us, influence and affluence never come and in themselves they rarely bring happiness. If you want to be great, Jesus told His disciples, you should seek to serve others (Matthew 20:25–27). Christ Himself had one purpose in life—to do the Father's will (Hebrews 10:7). He never became rich, but He was successful because His main goal in life was obedience to God.

All of this may sound theoretical, discouraging, and not very practical—especially as we seek to grow in our careers. There is nothing wrong with having high aspirations or wanting to do a good job in our vocations, but the Christian must keep aware of the biblical teachings about work. That is both realistic and practical.

Our vocations influence a lot more than the hours we work or the amount of money we earn. Where we live, the people we have as friends, our life-styles, how we spend our leisure time, even our place of worship can be influenced by the job. For the young adult, then, it is important to find an occupation and launch a career. If you are like many of your friends, you might make one or several vocational changes before settling into a more permanent line of work. You will also be deciding about extra education, learning more about your interests or abilities, and facing the tensions of on-the-job training.

Many people have no choice but to move into whatever work is available. Your career is likely to be more satisfying, however, if you can plan ahead and choose your occupation before starting to build a career.

Finding an Occupation

Have you ever wondered how your grandparents chose their lines of work? It has been suggested that people in the past reached their late teens or early twenties, made a relatively firm decision based on family expectations or available opportunities, settled into their life work without much further thought, and stayed there until retirement. In many parts of the world, this is still how job decisions are made.

Finding an occupation is not that simple for us. Most people think about their life work for a long time, and many of us struggle for several years to sort out our interests, abilities, goals, preferences, and opportunities. We start exploring different job possibilities almost from childhood and continue through the high school years. In college, we often take a variety of introductory courses and then settle on a major. The nonstudent often tries several jobs before focusing on a more specific line of work.

As a result of this exploration, we begin to discover the benefits and disadvantages of different kinds of work. We begin to see where we might fit and are able to reject a number of vocations for which we clearly are not suited. Our real interests and abilities become clearer, and we are faced with the realization that most of the fulfilling and rewarding jobs require a period of training. For some people, all of this exploration is done casually, without much planning or thought. For others there is vacillation, and a willingness to let circumstances direct their careers. Then there are those who try to plan their careers more rationally, giving thought to their own abilities and exploring the world of work more systematically.

If you are a more systematic planner, you might want to write down answers to the following questions. Ask a friend who knows you well to look over your answers and to give his or her opinion about what you wrote.

- What are my major areas of interest?
- What are my gifts and special abilities?
- What do I want in a vocation: fulfillment, a good income, travel, an opportunity to help others, contact with people, good fringe benefits, a place to use my talents, a place to serve God in a special way, prestige, opportunity for advancement, etc.? (List your preferences in their order of importance.)

- What kinds of work can best fit with my abilities and desires?
- What training would I need to enter my preferred line of work? (If you don't know, where could you get this information? Could your local library help?)
- What opportunities are available? Am I looking at an over-crowded career field, or at a vocation that is open to only a few people who have special education or abilities?
- What do my parents and close friends think about my choice of work? Do I agree with their assessment? Why?
- If I could plan my life, what kind of a person would I be and what work would I like to be doing ten years from today?

As you answer these questions, you probably will realize that your values, motives, past experiences, talents, beliefs, insecurities, hopes, personality traits, goals, and life dream (if you have one) can all have an influence on your choice of career. The Christian, however, has another issue to consider: What does God want me to do with my life?

In a lengthy and award-winning book, Edith Schaeffer wrote how she and her husband had seen God guide as they developed L'Abri, their spiritual center in the Swiss Alps, and as they each entered a worldwide ministry of speaking and writing. In *The Tapestry* she wrote:

> We had been living by prayer in a very vivid way, trusting the Lord to show us literally hour by hour what to do, where to go, and to provide the means. . . . But we *couldn't* have been clever enough to organize all that fell into place so quickly as we started to pray for God to unfold His will, as well as to send the people of His choice to us, and to supply the material needs. We were asking one basic thing, that this work would be a demonstration of God's existence. . . .
>
> What were our "visions" or "expectations" or "goals"? Simply a desire to demonstrate the existence of God by our lives and our work. . . . God is very patient and gentle with His children, as in a real measure . . . they attempt to live in close communication with Him, asking for help, asking for strength, depending on His wis-

dom and power rather than on their own cleverness and zip! . . .

We continued to live moment by moment, having things to be thankful for, things to rejoice about with excitement, things to regret and ask forgiveness for. We wept, we laughed, we thrilled, we agonized, we squealed with surprise. Reality is not a flat plateau. . . .

We especially asked that *our* lives would be a demonstration of *His* existence, in some small way, and not of *our* own strength.

Within recent years there has been a lot of talk about management by objectives. People are encouraged to set goals for their lives or businesses and to work step by step toward the attainment of these goals. But the Schaeffers didn't build L'Abri using objectives. Instead, they chose to let God lead while they sought divine guidance over every decision in their lives and work. Their example surely is a challenge to anyone who seeks to make decisions—including vocational decisions—that are consistent with God's will. Do we wait for divine leading, "trusting the Lord to show us literally hour by hour what to do . . . asking for help, asking for strength, depending on his wisdom and power" rather than on our "own cleverness and zip"? Do we set priorities and work toward them? Can we do both?

Surely, like the Schaeffers, we should seek to honor God in everything we do, trusting Him to guide in our lives. At the same time, again like the Schaeffers, we can use our God-given brains to make decisions that are consistent both with biblical teaching and with good principles of logic. It would be wrong, for example, to work in a career that stimulates immorality, takes advantage of people, or is characterized by deception and dishonesty. These are clearly inconsistent with biblical teaching. But there are many "honest" careers, where we can honor Christ by our competence and diligence, and where we can use our minds to set priorities and to make the best possible decisions about the future.

A former student once sent me a note that expressed a common dilemma. "I have received two excellent job offers," he wrote. "After weighing all (and I do mean all) the facts, and seeking counsel, I have decided that all the pros and cons balance out equally.

My feelings don't seem to lead either way, and after a lot of prayer, I don't feel any sense of direction. How do I make a decision?"

In all seriousness, I suggested that this man could flip a coin, start moving in one direction, and assume that God would make it clear if He wanted something different. Apparently both of the alternatives were desirable and neither conflicted with scriptural teaching. At a time like this, we can trust God to lead, ask Him to guide, and then make decisions based on the available evidence and on our best thinking. In His wisdom, God did not make human beings to be nonthinking robots. He gave us minds to be used and when we want to serve Him, He will lead, whether we sense this or not.

Building a Career

H.L. Wilensky has defined a career as "a succession of related jobs, arranged in a hierarchy of prestige, through which persons move in an ordered (more-or-less predictable) sequence." This formal-sounding statement expresses what most of us have seen, maybe even in ourselves: a common tendency, during a lifetime, for people to change jobs periodically, with the hope that each new position will be better than the one before.

Once we have found some suitable employment, it is easy to "get into the rut" of going to work, doing the minimum that is required, collecting our paychecks at week's end, and going home to more interesting activities. Such an attitude does nothing to advance our careers and neither does it honor Christ. "Whatever you do," the Bible tells us, "work at it with all your heart, as working for the Lord, not for men. . . . It is the Lord Christ you are serving" (Colossians 3:23, 24 NIV).

The more diligent worker strives to do a good job and gives some thought to career management. This involves making an effort to get along with others at work, learning to cooperate with superiors, improving one's skills or knowledge, and working toward personal and vocational goals.

The longer you remain in the work force, the harder it is to make career shifts. One survey found that 42 percent of the people questioned felt trapped in their jobs and unable to move to something as good or better. At times most of us feel frustrated with our work, and it isn't easy to stay at a job where we are not appreciated. When we are young, however, it is a little easier to make a move. You have fewer fringe benefits to give up if you move, fewer family responsibilities to keep you in one place, and more job opportunities. Even society looks on with acceptance and often approval if you pull up stakes once or several times during your twenties and move into something new.

According to Dr. Daniel Levinson and his research colleagues at Yale, this career building (even with the moves) can be greatly helped if you find a "mentor" to guide you into the world of work. A mentor is someone, usually a few years older, who has greater experience and seniority in the field of work that you are entering. Although a mentor can be a stranger who is admired from a distance, most mentors are people we know, perhaps eight to fifteen years older than us, who are willing to spend time guiding us into our careers.

The ideal mentor should act as a teacher who helps the younger person learn skills and acquire useful information, a model who serves as an example of someone who is already in the field, a counselor who gives encouragement and moral support, a sponsor who helps another get introduced to the occupation, and a guide who initiates the protégé into the customs, language, values, ethics, and people in the field. If you can find a good mentor, your entrance into a career is made a lot smoother.

However, mentors sometimes get threatened by the emerging competence of their protégés. There is a weakening of the strong, positive feelings and even love that once existed, and in time there may even be some competition. Bitterness and anger sometimes follow, but this doesn't have to happen. As you find your place in the field, you are less in need of a mentor. If he or she can then let go and encourage you to grow on your own, you will have a friend who is now a peer, and one to whom you can always remain grateful.

As you work with your mentor and grow into your career, you probably will make some initial decisions about an issue facing

Christians who are involved in career building: the question of success. We have been described by Joan L. Guest as "a nation of individuals relentlessly pursuing success." This pursuit drives millions in a quest for status, money, and power.

There is nothing wrong with being successful in one's field. It is an admirable goal to be competent in our work, to do the best job possible. The problem comes when our whole lives are geared toward avoiding failure, being recognized, and driving to get ahead.

For some reason, many people have concluded that only those who succeed are really worthwhile people. We have difficulty separating who we are from what we have accomplished. If we fail in our work we assume that we are failures as people—even though the Creator declared that His creatures are valuable regardless of our success or failure at work.

This drive for success is costly. Hundreds of magazine articles have described the ulcer-prone, stress-dominated lives of workaholics, but many keep driving nevertheless. In some occupations there is little freedom to do otherwise. But when work dominates our lives and consumes our thinking, it becomes a god. When possessions become too important, we can succumb to the love of money that is described in the Bible as the root of all evil (1 Timothy 6:10). We can forget that it is God "who richly provides us with everything for our enjoyment" and commands us "to do good, to be rich in good deeds, and to be generous and willing to share" (1 Timothy 6:17, 18). Prestige and acclaim, if they become important, can lead to pride and even create insecurity as we struggle to squelch our competitors and to stay at the top of our fields.

Several years ago a delightful little book appeared, called *Hope for the Flowers,* by Trina Paulus, describing the story of a caterpillar who discovered a pile of other caterpillars all squirming and pushing to climb a big caterpillar tower. The hero of this story joined the climb, stepping on other caterpillars and pushing to get to the top. When he got there he found nothing, although he spotted a few butterflies that seemed beautiful and free of the mass of caterpillars struggling to knock each other off the pedestal. Disappointed, the caterpillar hero went down from the pile, eventually spun a cocoon, and in time became the butterfly that it was meant to be.

This simple yet profound book has sold thousands of copies, perhaps because it is so relevant. In the climb to get ahead, we can cease to be what God intended and instead find ourselves pushing other human beings aside in our struggle to get to the top.

If you read Hebrews 11, you will notice that the heroes of the Bible were rarely social climbers. They were people who gave their lives to God and trusted that He would lead His children to develop their fullest potential, without hurting others. This is difficult to put into practice, especially if you are in a competitive line of work. In such occupations you do need drive, ambition, and persistence. But recognize, too, that God has given each of us gifts, strengths, and abilities that should be used to serve and honor Him. How you do this, without getting caught into the worldly drive for success, may be one of the most persistent issues that you will face as you build and live out your career.

Making Changes

Only in fairy tales do people make decisions and "live happily ever after." Finding an occupation and building a career can be stimulating activities, but there is no guarantee that our work will continue indefinitely and without interruption. Some very promising careers are halted abruptly by illness or accidents. Thousands of people with good educations and high motivation have had their career hopes dashed by an inability to find work that matches their capabilities. Economists call these the "underemployed." Others discover that unreasonable employers or hard-nosed professors can squelch professional progress, and even dedicated workers may be affected by economic trends or by a government's decision to require military service.

Each of these hindrances can create insecurity, loss of self-esteem, and depression. Each of these obstacles can bring financial pressure. If your former job was fulfilling, or if your career choice was exciting, you may find yourself grieving over a lost career.

Unemployment forces us to look carefully at our dreams and vocational goals. Even if you are in a secure position, however, there is value in periodically taking what has been called by Bridgford Hunt a "career audit." Ask yourself:

- Is this work or this job where I want to remain for the rest of my life?
- Have I already fallen into the success mentality so that I am more interested about getting ahead in my work than in serving the Lord with my life?
- Are my gifts, interests, and abilities being used where I am now working? If not, is a change feasible?
- What would I be giving up and what would I gain if I shifted jobs or changed careers at this time in life?
- What training or other education would I need to enter a new field?
- What practical steps must be taken if I change?
- Can I try out the new career without quitting my current job?
- How would my friends and family respond to my making a change?
- Would my new position honor Christ?
- Am I willing to pray about my decision and seek God's leading for this possible change in careers?

If you make the change, and perhaps even if you stay with your present position, at some time you might be faced with the need to make a move geographically, according to Naomi Golan in *Passing Through Transitions.* That can be exciting, but it also creates some new challenges as you make the transition to a new location.

Moves can be local (in the same community) or long-distance. They can be anticipated and planned, or they can be forced on us by a landlord or an employer who wants us to move. Some moves are temporary, as when a student goes to college for a few years, but other moves are permanent. Many moves are pleasant shifts to better jobs or communities, but sometimes people move "downward" because they have lost a house, a marriage, or an income. Some moves are minor relocations to some new nearby residence, while others involve the trauma of shifting many miles to a completely foreign and strange culture.

It has been suggested that moving involves four stages. First you make the decision. If this is a job-related move, you probably hope for a better position if you relocate. If the move involves a promotion, you may be more willing to go than if you are taking the risk of moving in the hope that you might find more job opportunities in some other community.

After you make the decision, you begin the stage of getting ready and breaking ties with your old community. If you are glad to go, this separation might be easier, but if you have friends and family in the old community, the prospect of leaving can bring both sadness and anxiety. Sometimes the busyness of getting ready is a protection that keeps you from facing the full impact of the coming change.

The stage of actually traveling to the new location can involve feelings of relief that everything has been packed and good-byes have been said, sadness about leaving your friends and the old familiar community, anxiety about what you might find in the new location, and excitement about the future.

Eventually, you start the stage of readjustment. Almost always there are some surprises when you move and sometimes a big gap exists between what you expected and what you find. Finding new friends, places to shop, housing, a doctor and dentist, a good church—these can all take effort and create stress. If you have a few possessions, if you move often, or if you enjoy moving, the adjustment may be easier. Even so, some time will pass before you feel part of a new community.

Facing Vocational Realities

In seminars for young adults, more questions are raised about careers than about any other single issue. Some of these are very insightful and point to realities that young adults face during the career-launching stage of life. Could any of the following questions have been written by you?

I'm struggling with whether to enter a secular career or to go into the ministry. Which is right for me?

I'm about to graduate from college. For twenty-two years my goal has been to finish college. Now what?

> Out of college for a few years, I don't have exact career goals but I feel many of my friends do. I'm torn between wanting to sort out the confusion and getting on with life or further schooling. I feel strange and a bit inferior because I don't have this all figured out already.

> I'm satisfied with the way my life is going. I don't seem to have problems except for this: How do I go through life doing what I'm doing but still be satisfied? Is there something else I should be doing? Is this all there is? Should I be satisfied?

I once asked a business executive if he was satisfied with his career. "Of course not," he replied. "If I were satisfied, I wouldn't be successful."

Throughout life it can be helpful to take those career audits, rethinking your priorities and asking God to keep you alert to His leading. In Psalms 37:34 David encouraged his readers, "Don't be impatient for the Lord to act! Keep traveling steadily along his pathway and in due season he will honor you with every blessing . . ." (TLB).

Instead of worrying or trying to jump impulsively from career to career, it is better to keep "traveling steadily" in your present job while you ponder your future directions. Ask God to give wisdom before you make any moves, and discuss your career periodically with someone who knows you well. If you, as a Christian, are diligent, available, and willing to be used by God, in His place of service, then you can know that He will work in and through your life, giving the degree of success and exposure that He wants you to have.

As you ponder this, you might also consider the problems of advancement in a career. You may share some of the concerns of the person who asked:

> How do I deal with the business world, building my career, and at the same time keep my Christian values? Politics, fear, and competition are all present at work. Doing my job well apparently isn't enough. I have to learn to play games if I am to survive.

It never is easy to make ethical decisions, especially when you are dealing with areas that the Bible never mentions. The opinions of friends can help, and so can their prayers. It also can be valuable to ponder what Jesus might have done in your present situation. Of course He lived in a different culture and period of history. The people in Nazareth never faced the pressures of today's business or professional world, but one thing we do know: Jesus, the One who is our example, would have decided what is right, then He would have done it.

Could that response apply to the next question?

> Much has been said about career advancement in corporations, but what about fields such as nursing, skill work, the pastorate, being a homemaker? There is less "climb the ladder" atmosphere in these jobs, but how do such people, including me, measure their progress and growth?

It isn't easy to measure success, especially when there are no bosses to tell us how we are doing. When I write a book, I sit alone in this little office and wonder if my work is poor, acceptable, or good. In a few years, after the book has been out for a while, I might see some reviews, but that doesn't help now, at the time when I work to write the words.

To keep going, I ask God daily to give me the desire and the ability to do a good job. I don't spend much time comparing my work with that of others, but I do try to improve on my own past performance. My goal is to make this manuscript better than the last. By competing with myself, I don't hurt anybody and I am motivated to keep improving.

> All of this talk about career management is fine but it overlooks my problem, which is one of relaxation. How do I balance my work with my need for leisure? I tend to be a workaholic, who is too busy to rest.

It is easy to let our lives get out of balance, to get caught up in work, and to forget our families and the need for relaxation. The problem is especially acute if you work for a company that expects your total commitment, if you are in a job where there literally is no time for leisure, or if you are in a ministry or other profession where you believe in the importance of "giving your all" for the work.

Most busy people know that they should slow down. The problem comes in turning this knowledge into action. Too often we become what Bruce A. Baldwin has called "leisure avoiders," who give lip service to the idea of slowing down but do nothing about it; we become "leisure blenders," who take time to relax but who always seem to mix this with work, squeezing a mini-vacation into a business trip, for example, or looking for business contacts even when on vacation; or we are "leisure ruminators," who actually take time off but who never forget the work we left behind. Maybe you don't fit into any of these three categories, but it is sobering to realize how easily people develop these ways of thinking as they get more involved in their careers.

How do you separate work from leisure and keep from slipping into the workaholic mentality?

Start by pondering the real value of relaxation. Leisure isn't simply fun. It is a necessary part of life. We need time for leisure if we hope to build relationships, manage stress, avoid burnout, and increase the overall productivity and quality of our work. Even Jesus took time to relax from His busy schedule. God created the world in six days and rested on the seventh. Who are we to think that all work and no play is healthy? Perhaps leisure is especially needed when the work load is heavy and you feel under pressure.

Once you are convinced that rejuvenation is important, set aside regular periods to relax. Don't try to schedule large blocks of time, at least when you begin. If the leisure time period is too big, you will be tempted to abandon your plan quickly. Instead, begin with smaller amounts of time and try to increase this later.

Then, recognize that relaxation is not meant to be a goal-directed activity. Some people decide to relax by getting involved with sports, but when they start competing with themselves or others, the "relaxation" has become another source of pressure. The people who have most trouble relaxing are often those who like competition, evaluations of performance, planning for the future, and making things happen. If these attitudes are allowed to intrude on your leisure times, you have undercut what relaxation is supposed to accomplish. Try, then, to experience things—like a sunset, a sauna, a swim—without analyzing them.

As you move in this direction, expect and confront uncomfortable feelings. It is common to feel guilty, self-condemning, or anxious. Ask God to help you resist these attitudes. Remember that leisure time serves a useful purpose and is consistent with Christian commitment.

Learning to relax, choosing a vocation, building a career, handling the changes that our jobs demand, and facing the realities of our work, can all be challenging, fulfilling, and frustrating. God gave us the responsibility to work diligently, but He also showed us that work must not dominate our lives—even when we are young and just getting started.

As you ponder your career, you might remember these words of John Wanamaker: "People who cannot find time for recreation are obliged sooner or later to find time for illness," and, we might add, ultimate failure.

Sooner or later we all think about money. How do you rate yourself at handling it?

A. I get by, could always use more.
B. No problem, have all I need, do what I want.
C. I'm one short step from food stamps, one giant leap from being solvent.
D. Money? Who worries about money? Master-Card, I'd follow you anywhere!

If you landed in the general vicinity of C or D, the following section is must reading. If you came out somewhere around A, you could still find some very valuable tips and new information. And if you're in the exclusive minority who would fit into the "money is no problem" category, it might be that most of what follows is old stuff. The point is, however, that a good manager is always interested in learning more. And there is always the challenge to be a better steward. As Winston Churchill said, "We make a living by what we get, but we make a life by what we give."

7

Making Ends Meet—When They Don't

From *Single* by Marilyn McGinnis

The love of money is the root of all evil. And the management of money isn't far behind. As the saying goes, "Why is there always so much month left at the end of the money?" Seems like no matter how you try, there's never enough money to meet all your expenses. Today's inflationary prices aren't helping any.

The best way to find out where your money goes is to do a little paperwork. Make a list of all of your expenses—weekly, monthly, and yearly. Include your rent, church and charity giving, food, automobile, insurance, clothing, recreation, gifts, and other items. Total your expenses for an entire year and then divide by twelve to determine how much you are spending month by month.

The next step is to work out a reasonable budget. If you don't *plan* how your money is to be spent, your expenses will fall into place of their own accord. Instead of you controlling your expenses, however, your expenses will end up controlling you.

Let's look at some of the major items in your budget.

Tithe. The first place to begin when you set up your budget is with the money you choose to return to the Lord. All that you have is a gift from Him. The Bible makes very clear that under the law, one-tenth of all that you have belongs to Him. It does not belong to you. And to hang onto it is to actually rob from God.

However, since we are under grace rather than law, a tenth is the very least we should give to God. What you give over and above a tithe is real giving. If you give grudgingly, out of a sense of duty, you might as well not give at all, for "God loves a cheerful giver." Once you decide to put God first in your giving, you will probably find it easier to put Him first in other areas of your life as well.

Savings. Force yourself to save or you will never save a cent. I know from experience how easy it is to let money slip through your fingers on things that seem so very worthwhile at the time. And in a year or so you have little to show for your spending except a collection of debts. Just as you set aside a tenth (or more) of your income for God, deduct another 10 percent for your savings account. Figure the rest of your budget within the remaining 80 percent.

Rent. One of the largest chunks of your income will probably be what you spend on rent. If you grew up in a very nice home, you will no doubt want at least the same standard of living when you venture out on your own for the first time. But remember, your earning power at age eighteen or twenty-two will probably in no way be comparable to that of your middle-aged father, who has worked for years to reach his present standard of living. A plush apartment for which you pay through the nose is hardly a wise investment of your money. A roommate to share expenses with is usually the best way to make ends meet.

As time goes on you may decide that you'd like to invest that rent money in property you can call your own. A condominium might be a good investment if you'd rather not have to worry about upkeep.

Select carefully the area in which you will live. Don't choose a house or apartment in an area of the city that is especially unsafe, just because the rent is cheap. And while we're talking about safety, let me suggest a few things I think are especially important for the single woman.

The next time you hear of a woman being beaten, raped, or murdered, read all you can about the incident. This may sound like a sordid assignment, but there's a reason for it. In almost every newspaper account I've read (if not all of them) the reporter has mentioned some precaution the woman failed to take. She left a bedroom window wide open. Or she left the door unlocked. She went for a walk in the park alone late at night. Or she left a shopping mall alone at night and jumped into her unlocked car without checking the backseat. Read—and profit from the mistakes of others.

Be sure your apartment is reasonably burglar proof before you move in. Second-floor apartments make window breaking more difficult than ground-floor apartments, unless a walkway runs the full length of the building. Do the windows have screens that lock? Do the windows lock tightly? One apartment I lived in for several months had a louvered glass window a few inches from the front door. All it took to break in (and I did it many times when I didn't have my key) was to slip out the screen, remove one louver, reach in, and twist the doorknob. If at all possible, have a night latch on every outside door and a peephole so you can look out but nobody can look in.

Keep your apartment or house locked when you're in it as well as when you're away. If it's too hot in the summer to keep the doors closed, find an apartment with screen doors that lock. A locked screen door lets the air in and at least puts up a temporary block for a burglar. Close and lock the door before you go to bed.

Never open your door at night unless you know who is on the outside. And it had better be someone you know well—your mother, your best friend, your minister. Don't let a salesman get one foot in the door. Many an unsuspecting woman has been raped, beaten, or even murdered simply because she opened a door she should have kept closed. Ask your friends to telephone before they come over.

If an intruder enters your home or apartment during the night, your best bet is usually to pretend to be asleep. If a man is there to molest you, however, you may have to use other tactics. One girl I read about calmly talked to the man. She kept up a steady dialogue, appealing to his pride by asking why such a good-looking man as he had to go around breaking into homes. The more she talked the more his passion subsided, and he finally left the house without harming her.

Never list your first name in the telephone directory. Use one or both initials. A single woman's name listed openly in the phone directory makes her a prey to any phone nut who decides to dial her number. And don't forget—if he has your phone number he also has your address. If you list only your initials you may end up on the mailing list of every men's clothing store in town. But throwing away junk mail is easier than trying to trace crank phone calls.

Be careful to whom you give your address and phone number. One woman I know joined a social group and let her name and address be placed in the group's printed directory. She was horrified one day to find the directory tacked to a telephone pole at a bus stop. Shortly after that a man caught her as she was going into her apartment and forced his way in. As calmly as possible she let him sit down and began to talk to him in an attempt to sidetrack him from his obvious intent. He told her many things about herself that a stranger wouldn't ordinarily know. Fortunately somebody scared him away before he did any harm. But the woman felt sure he must have found her through the bus stop copy or another copy of that directory.

When you join any kind of a group, be sure you know the purpose and membership well before you allow your name to be placed in a directory. Even then you can't control who gets a copy of that directory.

Never put your first name on your mailbox. List only your last name or initials and last name.

Food. Your health is your most important possession and what you eat determines in large measure just how healthy you will be. If you're constantly on the go, the line of least resistance is to skip a meal, grab a snack here and there, or live on a diet of hamburgers and coffee. If you live alone, there usually isn't much incentive to fix first-rate meals just for yourself.

Eating in restaurants all the time is pretty expensive and robs you of the opportunity to learn how to be a really good cook. Force yourself to fix and eat well-balanced meals. With careful planning you can eat well on even a small food budget.

Automobile. One of the most expensive items in your budget is your automobile—if you own one. Owning and operating a car is a big investment, and the cost will probably continue to climb.

Before you jump into any car purchase, ask yourself if you really need one. If you live in a city where mass transit is available, an automobile may be an unnecessary luxury you really can't afford.

Total up the amount of money you spend per month on gas and oil, car payments, insurance and repairs, and you will discover that a large portion of your paycheck is eaten up by your car. Consider the possibility of selling your car and using the bus.

Think through the areas of the city where you travel the most and study the bus or subway lines that serve those areas. Then find an apartment that is close to one of those lines and also close to shopping and laundry facilities. The few times you really need a car you can always rent one. Although the cost of renting a car may be high, you will save money in the long run.

If you do not know how to drive, by all means take driving lessons and learn how. I think it is very important for a woman to be able to drive. This is one area where being a "helpless Hannah" is not necessarily a good idea. Emergency situations may arise when it is essential that you know how to drive.

Selecting a car is often difficult for a single woman—particularly if you are buying a used car. Those of us who buy cars by color, size, or the number of accessories often learn to our dismay that what's up front is a lot more important than the paint job.

Don't buy a big fancy car unless you are rolling in money. A big car whose maintenance cost is high and gas mileage low is a poor investment and will keep you perpetually broke. Stick to the smaller and less expensive compact cars that are cheaper to operate.

When you buy a car, especially a used car, take someone with you who understands the inner workings of the automobile. Your father, brother, or a friend will probably be glad to help you select a model that runs well and is within your budget.

To help you purchase a new car at a reasonable price, an organization called Car/Puter International Corp. (1603 Bushwick Avenue, Brooklyn, New York 11207—1-800-221-4001 toll free or 1-718-455-2500 in New York metropolitan area) will be of help. For a data processing fee of $18 (plus 75¢ for postage and handling) Car/Puter will send you a detailed computerized printout listing both the dealer cost and the suggested retail price (sticker) for your specific car and for each factory option available. You can use the Car/Puter printout in one of three ways:

1. You may use the printout as a bargaining tool to assist you in negotiating the best possible purchase of your new car with any dealer of your choice. When considering the huge investment you are about to make, you really can't afford to be without this valuable and powerful information.
2. Purchase direct from a member dealer of the Car/Puter Dealer Group when a member dealer is listed on your printout. Simply contact that dealer for an appointment so that you may place your order. He will assist you in every way possible.
3. Purchase your car through the Car/Puter Referral Service when a dealer is not listed on your printout. You may still order your car through the Car/Puter Courtesy Delivery Service and take delivery from a new car dealer within your local area.

Learn something about your car. Take a course in auto mechanics (yes, women take them, too) or ask a friend for help. It won't strain your femininity to learn how to change the oil or a tire. Changing the oil will save you a little money, and knowing how to change a tire may come in mighty handy if you are stranded somewhere and nobody comes to your rescue.

One of the big costs of owning an automobile is auto insurance. Contact several insurance agencies and compare prices. Consider insurance costs before you buy a car. Your age, and the age, make, and model of the car are important factors. So is the area in which you live.

The bane of every woman car owner's existence is trying to find a reliable mechanic to repair her car. Since most of us know very little about automobiles, we are the prey of any unscrupulous mechanic who wants to make a fast buck (or a couple of hundred bucks!).

There is no sure way I know of to find a reliable mechanic except through trial and error. Here again, friends can be a help. Ask around and see who your friends recommend. Once you find a mechanic you can trust, stick with him till death do you part. A mechanic who sees you regularly will probably be less inclined to gyp you than one who has never seen you before and will never see you again.

When you travel, be especially careful of service station attendants who tell you that you need a new fan belt, your radiator cleaned out, or some other repair, when all you did was stop for gas. An attendant with a razor blade hidden between his fingers can slit your fan belt without your knowing it and then tell you that you need a new one. If he places two fingers below the handle when he inserts the dip stick, the oil mark will be lower on the stick than it should be. If you tell him to add oil, he may use a can that is actually empty—and charge you for the oil he didn't put in.

When you stop for gas or repairs, get out of the car and watch what goes on under the hood. You may not know a battery from a spark plug, but the mechanic doesn't know that. He'll be less inclined to pull any funnies if you're watching every move he makes. If he tells you something is definitely wrong with your car, thank him and then drive to another station or two for a consensus of opinion before you have work done.

And now for a few safety rules regarding the use of your car.

Always lock your car when it is parked and when you are in it. Even when you are driving in broad daylight, keep the doors locked. Always check the backseat of your car before getting in. Many tragedies occur when a woman carelessly hops into a car without checking the backseat, only to find, moments later, a gun at her neck or a hand on her shoulder.

Never walk anywhere alone at night in a big city—even on a well-lighted street. Go by car if your car is parked close to your apartment, or by bus if the bus stop is nearby. If neither of these is available, wait until daylight. Your safety is more important than whatever you thought you needed at the store.

Health Insurance. No matter how small your income, one item you must not overlook is health insurance. You may not enjoy paying the monthly premiums when you're in good health, but if you get sick you'll be mighty glad you did. If the company you work for does not provide health insurance, investigate a plan that meets your needs.

Life insurance. Who would pay the funeral expenses if you were to die tomorrow? Maybe you've never given that much thought, but it's time you did. A policy that at least covers burial expenses would be a big help to whoever becomes responsible for your affairs after your demise.

Additional Insight for Handling Finances

From *Getting Started* by Gary R. Collins

Long before we reach adulthood, most of us recognize that it isn't easy to handle money. The following are some general principles that others have found to be helpful.

1. Recognize that good money management involves a desire to manage money well, skills in knowing how to manage money, and a clear idea of one's values.

2. The Bible says a lot about money and possessions. Read the following passages and ask how they apply to you: Matthew 6:19–34; Deuteronomy 15:7–11; 1 Timothy 6:6–10, 17–19; James 2:1–7; 1 John 3:17, 18; Philippians 4:12, 19.

3. Ask God to help you with your finances.

4. Recognize that there is nothing wrong with money or possessions; what is wrong is the love of money and the drive to accumulate possessions.

5. It has been said that the amount of money you have is less important than the way in which your money is managed. Consider the following management suggestions:

- When you get your pay, try to put aside some money for savings, and some for God's work.
- Try to avoid borrowing or using credit cards, except in extreme emergencies.
- Take some time to set some financial objectives. What things are important to you?
- Rank your financial priorities. What do you want first? What are you willing to wait for?
- Avoid impulse buying—especially if you are being pressured by a salesperson. What is on sale at one time will probably be on sale again.
- Develop a spending plan. Write down your annual income, make a note of your giving and fixed income, and then estimate your expenses. Try to set a realistic budget and stick to it.
- Keep accurate records. That is time-consuming, but accurate records not only help at tax time, they also let you see where your money is going, how accurate your budget plan has been, and whether there is need for change.
6. Remember that everything we have is from God.
7. When things get financially difficult, remember that God does supply our needs.

Credit Buying

If your wallet looks anything like that of most people, you are well stocked with credit cards. In some ways they are a valuable piece of plastic. In many ways they are the curse of our society.

Credit cards are good for emergencies and for identification purposes. But for most of our buying they are a definite liability. Why? Because they encourage us to live far above our means.

A credit card allows you to:

buy what you can't afford
spend money you don't have and may never have (What if you get laid off?)
pay as much as 18 percent interest on unpaid balances
keep yourself continually in debt

If you use a credit card wisely it can be your friend. Never charge more than you can pay off in a lump sum when your next bill comes in. If you have to make a large purchase which you can't pay off all at once, take out a loan at a bank where the interest will be substantially lower than that charged by the department store. If you really want to put an end to splurge buying, tear up all of your credit cards except one. Save that one for identification purposes and for dire emergencies.

Retirement

At age twenty-five the idea of saving up and investing for your retirement may seem decidedly remote. Most of us figure that pretty soon we'll get married and then we won't have to worry about a retirement income. Friend husband will take care of all that.

But suppose you don't marry. Or you marry and are widowed with no provisions for your retirement. Financial planning at fifty-five or sixty is a little late. There are several ways you can plan for your retirement. Let's take a look at some.

Social security. A guaranteed income when you retire sounds like smooth sailing. But frequent articles in the newspapers indicate that it is just about impossible to live on social security alone. Therefore, it is vitally necessary that you make additional financial provisions for your retirement.

Pensions. When you take a job, inquire about the retirement plan provided by the company. Maybe you won't stay with the same company long enough to take advantage of its plan. But then again maybe you will.

Investments. One of the earliest ways to invest your money is through a mutual funds plan. You can invest a little or a lot and the company will handle your money for you. When you retire, your original investment plus the money it has made for you through the years is available to you in a lump sum or in monthly installments.

If you're interested in learning about the stock market, a number of books are available to help you tell the difference between the bulls and the bears. If you have only a small amount to invest, you might want to join an investment club where each person's money is pooled to buy shares and you learn how to buy. Talk to a stockbroker and ask him about an investment club you could join, or ask him to do your investing for you.

Savings. Consider your savings account as a cushion fund for the present and future, but not necessarily as a source of retirement income. The interest paid by a bank is low in comparison to the earning power your money will have if you invest.

These are a few of the retirement plans available. As you assess your financial future you will discover other ways. The important thing is to start planning now for your future.

Ten Money-Saving Tips

And now for a few tips on how to make and save a little money:

1. Do your Christmas shopping in January and August when the white sales are on. Watch other sales during the year, also, and you can do most of your gift buying at a fraction of the full price. Be sure the items you buy are something the person does not have or, if buying clothing, that the item will fit. Sale items usually can't be returned.

2. Buy clothing at the end of the season when it is on sale and save it for next year. Avoid extremely faddish items that may not be in style next year.

3. Clip coupons that offer 25¢ or more off or cash refunds on food and household items. Save the amount deducted from the price or you will never benefit from the coupons. I collect my "cold hard cash" coupon money in a jar in the refrigerator (if you were a burglar would you look in the refrigerator for money?) and use it primarily for birthday and Christmas presents.

4. One way to save money on your grocery bill is to comparison shop. However, this takes time that you as a working girl may not have. If you don't have time to shop in several stores, watch for sales and special discounts in the store where you do shop. For example, store brands are usually cheaper than name brands and taste

just as good. A large sign may announce that a certain name brand is on special for twenty-seven cents a can. Right next to it you discover the store brand is only twenty-five cents.

5. With the high price of meat you would do well to learn how to use some of the less expensive proteins. For example, cheese, canned tuna, and kidney beans provide necessary protein at considerably lower cost than expensive cuts of beef and pork.

6. Have a garage sale. Clean out all the old junk you want to get rid of: clothing, jewelry, furniture, dishes, etc. Put up a sign or run an ad in the newspaper. Ask friends and neighbors to go in with you if you don't have much to sell.

7. Take advantage of other people's garage and patio sales. Thrift stores are another source of good buys. Discipline yourself not to buy things you don't need just because they're cheap. Look for items you actually need and you'll be surprised how inexpensively you can furnish your apartment or clothe yourself.

8. If you're really in a financial bind, consider moonlighting, but only for a few hours or for a short period of time. If you work at a "think" job all day, choose a moonlight job that doesn't require much thinking. Don't moonlight for long. It isn't worth the damage to your health.

9. Turn a hobby into a profit maker. If needlecraft, pottery, or candlemaking is your specialty, perhaps your local handcraft shop will sell your things on consignment. If you've always wanted to be a writer or an artist, take some night classes and give it a try. Nothing ventured, nothing gained. You just might discover some hidden talent you didn't know you had.

10. Join a book club and take advantage of the introductory offer. Use the discount and introductory books for gifts or to build up your own library. Choose a club which has enough books you need or want to make joining worthwhile.

Live Below Your Means

A single friend suggests that instead of not living beyond your means you should not even live up to your means. In other words, don't spend every cent you have. Set your standard of living *below* what you actually could afford. In today's economy that isn't easy, but it is possible if you are willing to make some sacrifices here and there.

Why should you try to live below your means? She suggests several reasons. There is a sense of freedom in knowing that you could spend more if you wanted to. The person who barely scrapes by from paycheck to paycheck hardly feels secure. When you live below your means you then have opportunity to expand yourself as a person. Use the extra money for travel, preparation for retirement, music lessons, a lecture series, and for other things that are a worthwhile investment of your time and money.

This same friend tells of the time she had to leave her job out West for a job in the East. She did not look forward to the adjustment from a warm climate to a bitterly cold one. In fact she didn't want to take the job at all. But she knew that was where God wanted her and so she went. After she moved she bought herself a gift—a beautiful fur coat. And whenever people asked about her coat she told them it was "a gift to me from myself." While the coat represented a healthy investment, it was not money ill-spent. The coat was lighter weight and warmer than a cloth coat and outwore several cloth coats in the long run—plus the added factor of a pleasant boost to her morale. It matched everything and always looked elegant. The point is, however, she was obviously not living up to her means or she could never have afforded such a happy gift.

Perhaps this is a little of what Jesus meant when He told us, ". . . do not worry about your living,—what you are to eat (or drink), or about your body, what you are to wear" (Matthew 6:25 MLB). One of the ways God provides for us is by giving us the good sense to know how to manage our money. The person who barely makes it from payday to payday or lives beyond his means takes plenty of thought about what he will eat, drink, and wear. Worrying about your finances is time-consuming and an emotional drain. There will be times when all of us must give serious attention to our financial condition. But in the long run I think many of our worries could be eliminated if we actually lived below our means.

Put God first in every aspect of your financial affairs. Ask Him to give you the wisdom to manage your finances wisely. When I go shopping I frequently ask God to show me the things I should buy and keep me from buying the things I shouldn't. It's a great way to reduce frivolous spending.

Super Guide to Saving Money

From *Today's Christian Woman* Magazine

March/April 1984

by Melissa Aberle

Know When to Borrow

Deciding when to use credit is one of the most difficult financial dilemmas you'll face. Good stewards never become strapped by debts. But there are times when using credit makes sense. Here are six sensible guidelines for borrowing:

1. *Do* borrow for a needed item that you've found at an unusually low price. By charging it, putting it on a time-payment plan, or getting a low-cost loan, you'll be playing it smart. So, in the situation given above, buying the refrigerator on credit is a wise choice.

2. *Don't* buy on credit unless you have a reasonable prospect of repaying the loan at this time.

3. *Do* borrow to meet emergency needs for your family, such as health.

4. *Don't* use credit to increase your status or boost your morale. A weekend vacation "just because I need it" is fine if you can afford it. But find an inexpensive way to unwind if you don't have the ready cash.

5. *Don't* be lured into buying something you don't need because payment terms seem easy (for example, a TV set offered for one hundred dollars down with three years to pay off the rest).

6. *Do* borrow for education that you've evaluated as immediately beneficial and of long-range value. The value of education cannot be measured by the usual yardsticks.

Reducing Risk: How to
Choose Insurance

What takes a big chunk of your income, comes in as many varieties as Life Savers, and has been called "risk management"? It's insurance. Regardless of how much you earn, you will probably eventually get several kinds of insurance. But how do you decide how much you need, and when? Here's a list of the five major types of insurance, and the latest tips for choosing a policy that fits your needs.

Life. This insurance is the hardest to gauge correctly. You have to estimate foreseeable dollars with unknowable future events. If no one is relying on you for financial support, you probably don't need any life insurance at all. If you are someone's provider, you should estimate life insurance goals based on three things: your estimate of family's annual living expenses, the number of years that you want to provide for them, and the amount you plan to set aside for your children's college education.

You will choose between two types: *whole life,* a policy that doubles as a savings account; and *term life,* which provides nothing but protection. Whole life generally costs at least one thousand dollars a year for either a man or a woman.

Health. Your first choice in health (medical) insurance should be a policy through your place of employment or professional association, or a group plan. Outside of these options, you'll have higher yearly payments.

Most people choose a hospital policy plus a major-medical or medical-catastrophe policy. The latter takes care of hospital and doctor bills not covered by other policies.

Tips:

- Policies that cost much less may provide poor coverage. Avoid insurance promising to pay a set amount for each day in the hospital instead of a fixed portion of total expenses.
- If you're nearing retirement, you should buy a Blue Cross or commercial policy that pays most charges not covered by Medicare (which pays an average of only 50 percent of a retiree's health costs.)

Disability (Income Protection). The most valuable financial asset you have is your own earning power. Thus, if you support anyone financially, you must have disability insurance. Typically, a wage earner carrying this type of insurance will insure up to 60 percent of her income.

Tips:

- Select both accident and sickness disability coverage with lifetime benefits, if possible, and make sure that your policy is noncancelable and guaranteed renewable.
- Check with your employer to see if some kind of group income-protection insurance is available through the company.

Homeowner's. A homeowner's insurance policy is a comprehensive policy that covers your home and its contents. There are at least five different forms of homeowner's policies offered in most states. Choose one carefully that corresponds to your home and your budget.

Tips:

- Shop around for an insurance company. Rates and coverage are not identical with all companies. The reputation and service of the company is vital.
- The *premium* on insurance, the amount you must pay each year, is based partly on the size of the deductible you choose. This is the cost of damage you are willing to pay. (With a $100 deductible plan, if a portion of your roof is blown away, you pay the first one hundred dollars to get it fixed.)

The experts advise that you live with as large a deductible as you can. Premiums are not tax-deductible, but losses are deductible after the first one hundred dollars.

Automobile. Either the bank that gives you a loan or the state in which you live probably requires you to have liability insurance. Every car owner should have this policy, which covers your financial responsibilities in an accident seriously injuring another person.

A typical auto insurance policy is a package of several kinds of coverage. Besides liability, you should look into: collision, comprehensive physical damage, uninsured-motorist, and medical payments insurance.

Tips for keeping costs down:

- If you have teenage drivers your insurance costs can double. To reduce that cost, make sure they complete an approved course in driver's education.
- As with homeowner's insurance, choose a policy with a deductible larger than one hundred dollars. Your premiums will be lower, and you'll save in taxes.

A Shopper's Guide to
Financial Institutions

Shopping among financial institutions to decide what to do with your money, you might feel like a small-town girl visiting a big city supermarket. So you don't get lost in the aisles, here's a shopper's guide.

Commercial Banks. These offer the most services: savings programs, checking accounts, credit cards, mortgages, and loan programs. Traditionally, they haven't offered the best interest on savings. But since October 1982, when the government took its first step toward deregulating financial institutions, banks began offering higher interest.

Savings and Loan Associations. These institutions are allowed by law to pay slightly more interest than banks. This, too, is changing. By 1986 all financial institutions will be allowed to pay any interest.

Savings and Loans can also offer interest-bearing checking accounts, known as NOW or Negotiable Order of Withdrawal accounts. Most of these are free checking accounts, requiring a minimum balance.

Mutual Savings Banks. Found in only a few states, these are virtual duplicates of commercial banks.

Credit Unions. A credit union (CU) is a nonprofit savings and loan cooperative consisting of people with something in common: their place of employment, their union, their religion, profession, etc. Traditionally, CUs have offered reasonably priced loans and often higher interest on savings than other financial institutions.

While continuing to emphasize consumer loans and some financial counseling, CUs now offer a service very similar to checking called share draft accounts. Most of these accounts are free, and you use the share drafts as you would checks.

Tips:

- In every financial institution, each account under a different name should be insured. If you have any doubts about your institution's federal insurance, ask! On this, you should have no doubts whatsoever.
- The services offered by each institution are similar. Look for differences in:
  —the rates, incentives, and options of the services.
  —to whom the financial institution wants to appeal—large groups or corporations, small businesses, or individuals. Watch this distinction; you may get poor service from a bank simply because they're not set up to perform a particular service.

Part Three

—◆—

Keep Patching: In Tune With Our Sexuality

Sex and singleness is possibly the toughest subject this book will address. It's particularly difficult for those who choose to embrace the teachings of the Bible where the pattern for sexual expression is defined and narrow. It's easy, of course, to apply our own interpretations and nuances to those well-defined verses that deal with sex. We can be incredibly adept at making Scripture fit our particular sexual preferences, thus exonerating our guilt feelings while justifying our behavior. No question about it—the choice is there for us to make. Nobody ties our hands behind us and forces us to do what the Bible teaches. In that regard, we can say we have the right to do as we like. But the real question is this: are we prepared to live with the consequences of what we think is worth liking?

8

It's a Jungle Out There

From *Suddenly Single* by Jim Smoke

It was time for questions at the end of a singles seminar. A hand at the back of the room went up very slowly. As I pointed in that direction, a quavering voice stammered out the question: "Would you s-s-s-s-ay something about s-s-s-s-ex?" I responded by saying that sex was fun. Several laughed while others remained silent. I knew that wasn't the answer the questioner had desired. My second response was to acknowledge that this is a genuine problem for many single-again people. The audience breathed easier and nodded their heads in agreement.

Of all the issues I have been asked about by singles in recent years, the question of how to handle singleness and sexuality is the most frequent.

There seems to be an assumption afloat on the sea of singleness that after a person has been married and enjoyed a sexual relationship, when they become single again they simply can't live without sex. After watching a few TV soaps, daytime or evening variety, it would appear that one of life's great pastimes is playing musical beds. Many of those people jumping in and out are either divorced, about to be divorced, having an affair, or single. If we absorb what we witness on television long enough, we might be convinced that everyone lives that way.

A lady approached me on a Sunday morning at the end of our singles class. She stated that she was newly divorced and wanted to know why, as the word got out in her community, many of her former spouse's male friends were calling her and asking her if she had any "needs" they could help fulfill. (I hesitate to tell you what they really asked.) It may have happened to you. Her question was "Why?" I am not sure of the answer, but I have heard the question from many singles.

Sex and Sexuality

We could define sex or the sex act as a biological function. That is the level at which many people deal with it. On a higher level, we have to deal with sexuality as a total package. That package does not consist of just a biological function. It includes intimacy, love, feelings, consideration, kindness, caring, support, and trust. It involves one's whole emotional being. It is involvement with another person that is total and complete, and continues that way through life. This is not easy to come to grips with. Many people never get beyond shortsighted sex to understand the longer view and its involvements. Is your view and understanding of sexuality short-circuited by recognizing only the biological-need level?

Ours is a sex-saturated society. Much of today's advertising is tied to sexual identification. You are definitely out of step if you don't go with the stream of today's sexual thinking. Rather than just admitting it's a big problem and talking about something else, let's explore some of the reasons that lie behind the sexual issue.

Loneliness. Many singles have shared with me that they became sexually involved with another person just to eliminate their gripping loneliness for an evening. In the deep moments of the intimacy of a sexual relationship, their loneliness seemed to vanish. The problem is that it returns again after the experience ends. The supposed cure becomes, in effect, a Band-Aid for the problem.

We all know how good a hug feels when we are hurting. It makes us feel warm, cared for, accepted. A sexual encounter can bring about those same feelings, even temporarily. It can be a way of telling yourself that you are okay after all and that you won't be lonely anymore. But in the words of a popular song, "There's got to be a morning after." On that morning dawns the realization that you have only traded some of your loneliness for short-lived affection.

Desire to be loved. There is probably no better feeling than the knowledge that we are loved in significant ways by others. I meet many people who are love starved. They often reach out in frantic efforts for any kind of love.

In a marriage, everyone experiences some form of love from their mates. That love gives a feeling of security. In the world of the suddenly single, often after a severe rejection, there is a deep desire to prove that one is lovable.

There are many ways to feel loved without sexual involvement. There is an old saying: "Never replace the future on the altar of the immediate." Many singles seem to be going the instant-intimacy route in an effort to prove that they can be loved right now. Love in the future is too far away to wait for.

Manipulation and intimidation. "If I don't go to bed with him, he won't ask me out again." I have heard that statement hundreds of times from the single women I meet. It sounds like the threat of the hijacker who says to the pilot of the plane, "Fly me to Cuba, or I will explode this bomb." It's called intimidation, and our society has become expert at its usage. We hear it on all sides. Unions ask for more money and threaten to strike if they don't get it. We threaten to sue our neighbor if his dog doesn't stay off our lawn. We are living in a litigation-happy society. The message, in all areas, is "Give me what I want or I will punish you physically, emotionally, socially, mentally, or financially."

When a sexual encounter is traded for an evening on the town because of the fear that there will be no more evenings on the town, someone is being manipulated. The tragedy is that this can become a way of life. Sexual bartering is about as prevalent as window-shopping.

The victims of this sexual intimidation-manipulation game come away feeling used and conned. Their self-esteem goes begging in the process of having their feelings ignored.

Sexual rights. I have heard numerous single-again people say that they have a right to a sexual relationship with any consenting adult they choose. As a professor in my college used to say, "Your rights extend to the end of your nose." A sexual encounter involves two people. Do the rights of the other person supersede yours, or do yours supersede his?

Your rights and the rights of others are precious and guarded responsibilities. When someone uses you for his own gratification, your rights are being violated.

Self-gratification. Many sexual encounters are simply trips into self-gratification—looking out for yourself and stepping on others to fulfill your own needs. You hurt others so that you can be satisfied, and you try to catch the brass ring for yourself. How long can your needs be met at someone else's expense? Before long, the other person will feel hurt and used, and grow increasingly calloused toward you.

Most singles organizations have a problem with a group of wandering singles known as "body snatchers." They are the marauders who invade singles groups to satisfy their own sexual needs and experience another conquest.

I asked one woman how she handled an approach by a "body snatcher." She said, "I laugh a lot, look him in the eye and say, 'You've got to be kidding,' and walk away." This is probably the best reaction. And in case women readers are thinking that men are always the marauders, let me tell you that there are lots of women in the seducing business.

You may be thinking that this sounds like a description of a swinging-singles group you might read about in the newspaper. My experience has been that these problems exist in church-oriented singles groups everywhere. The only difference is that they are not talked about openly in a religiously oriented group.

Everyone is doing it. We live in an age of conscious collapse. We are easily seduced by the thought that "everyone is doing it," "everyone is buying it," "everyone is wearing it," and "everyone is going there." Clothing fads tell us to get into our signature jeans or we will be stared at when we go out. The insinuation is that we had better get with it or we will be out of step with the world.

This same mind set carries into the area of sexual involvement. Society says that everyone is having sex with everyone else and that you are quite abnormal if you don't participate. Group pressure to conform and not be left at the gate when the race starts begins to swallow you up.

You can't collect your standards from the crowd. They have to come from you, without external pressure. Absorbing others' views and standards leaves you never quite sure about yourself. No one enjoys living with uncertainties.

You are *you*. You are not everyone else!

Can't live without sex. I often listen to this myth as it is passed around singles groups. The logic seems to be that the sex drive and sexual fulfillment are human needs that must be met whether inside or outside of marriage.

I have met many singles who are celibate and have been that way for some years. They have made a choice for their single-now status. They are not strange-looking folks with little horns protruding from their ears. They are happy, growing people who have simply exercised their right to choose for themselves and are living that choice out.

Several recent magazines have reported a growing interest in celibacy for singles. It could well be that we have reached our saturation point in the sexual jungle, and some people are looking for more meaningful ways to handle their sexuality. No one is saying that this is easy, but neither is running a marathon. The end result is the important part.

Always remember that sex was made *for* man and woman, not man for sex.

Just talking about the reasons for conflict in the area of facing sex as a single-again person does not solve the problem. Many single-again people are looking for justification for what they want to do. Others are simply trying to decide what to do.

Three Attitudes Toward Dealing With the Sexual Struggle

Attitude one. Sex is okay—anytime, anyplace, with anyone who is a consenting adult and of legal age. Does that sound a little like the last television show you watched? Probably! This attitude is held by a large segment of the singles world today. It follows the slogan "If it feels good, do it." We could probably call this sexual liberty or sexual freedom. We forget that freedom always comes with responsibilities attached. In the world of sexual license, there are seldom thoughts of responsibilities. This is, at best, random sex.

Attitude two. Sex is okay—anytime, anyplace, with anyone of legal age, but only if you have a "meaningful relationship" with the person. The question that arises here is, "What does *meaningful* mean?" It is a relative term. If I said I had a meaningful breakfast this morning, would you know what I had? It could be two vitamins and a glass of juice, or the whole breakfast special at my neighborhood restaurant. What is known as meaningful to one person may lack meaning to another person.

Meaningful in the above context could mean you have had three dates with the same person before you engage in sex. It could mean sixty dates. It could mean engagement.

Some people would call this selective sex. Many singles find themselves in this situation. They don't want to be known as bed hoppers, so they opt for a smattering of involvement to justify a sexual relationship.

Attitude three. Sex is a gift from God, and it comes with great responsibility to the participants. It is best enjoyed to its fullest within the context of a marital relationship. Sounds rather restrictive, doesn't it? You might wonder if anyone in today's world really believes this. Contrary to what you might think, there are many single-again persons who believe that this attitude is the right one for them and seek to live by it.

These three attitudes are widely scattered throughout the singles community. Let me ask you several questions to help you sharpen your own focus:

1. Which one of the three attitudes describes where you are in your own thinking right now? Be honest.
2. How did you arrive at that attitude? What led you to it and what or who influenced you?
3. Is it the best and right place for you to be? Why?
4. Where do you think God wants you to be? Why?

What I have discovered from talking to thousands of single people about this subject is that many of them have never really thought much about where they stand. They have developed a conditional stand, a sort of "We'll see what happens and what kind of opportunities come up, then decide." Living by situation ethics is always precarious. You never have a solid foundation under you. You are totally subject to your emotions of the moment. It's a little like standing on a cloud.

I believe that people with well-thought-through convictions draw respect. People who live in the cracks of life are never taken too seriously.

The above questions will provide you with a lot of homework. If you do it, you will find your struggles in this area greatly reduced.

What Does God Think About Sex and Singleness?

That's a good question, and many people don't want to know. If you have decided to follow God, then you need to know and wrestle with the implications.

The Scriptures talk about a general principle for all our behavior in 1 Corinthians 10:31: "So, whether you eat or drink, or whatever you do, do all to the glory of God" (RSV). The "whatever" is pretty comprehensive. It includes relating sexually in your life. Most people would not think that. They would look at the obvious things like fun, hobbies, conversation, and jobs. Paul put the *all* in there for our own safety in making decisions.

Some years ago, a friend suggested that I always consider two questions when I had to make a decision in my life. The first was, "Can this be done to the glory of God?" The second was, "Is this the best that God intends for me?" When those two questions are used in the sexual-involvement evaluation, you might come to some rapid solutions in dealing with the issue.

In a more specific way, Paul speaks again in 1 Corinthians 6:13–20 RSV. He starts by talking about food again. I guess he knew that would get our attention every time:

"Food is meant for the stomach and the stomach for food"—and God will destroy both one and the other. The body is not meant for immorality, but for the Lord, and the Lord for the body. And God raised the Lord and will also raise us up by his power. Do you not know that your bodies are members of Christ? Shall I therefore take the members of Christ and make them members of a prostitute? Never! Do you not know that he who joins himself to a prostitute becomes one body with her? For, as it is written, "The two shall become one flesh." But he who is united to the Lord becomes one spirit with him. Shun immorality. Every other sin which a man commits is outside the body; but the immoral man sins against his own body. Do you not know that your body is a temple of the Holy Spirit within you, which you have from God? You are not your own; you were bought with a price. So glorify God in your body.

These are some of the strongest words Paul spoke regarding the use of our bodies. The people in his day faced the same issues and struggles that we face today. The only difference between Paul's time and ours is that we get better media coverage.

The single-again Christian listens to the logic the world offers in the sexual area. She battles with her own emotions and feelings, but must still measure them against what the Scriptures teach. It is only then that answers begin to become clear.

A Christian's sexual ethics and conduct need to be determined by the understanding of what God really had in mind when He gave man and woman the gift of sex. This gift was certainly a great idea. It was given for enjoyment and pleasure as well as procreation. But it was also given in trust. The trust was that it would be used within the boundaries that God intended for it to be used. I believe the Scriptures are clear in stating that those boundaries are within the framework of the marriage relationship.

That does not mean that having a sexual relationship outside of marriage is not fun. It does mean that it will never bring you God's intended best in the way of enjoyment and fulfillment. Perhaps this is why so many sexually worn-out singles ask me if there is some other answer in this area that they missed along the way.

God knew what He was doing when He designed men and women. It's only when we try to do the redesigning that we get into trouble. Getting mad at God because you don't like His design, and doing your own thing will not bring you happiness.

Sex is a choice, and choices always bring responsibilities. As a single-again person, you won't be around too long before you are confronted with the sexual issue. Your own rationalizing may click into gear before you have a chance to check into God's best intentions. Your own needs, desires, feelings, frustrations, and lack of love and loving may dominate your thinking. Let me share several suggestions for you to think about as you work to resolve this issue.

1. Really check out for yourself what the Scriptures teach. Read the references and commentaries.
2. Read a few good books that deal expansively with sexuality, singleness, and marriage.
3. Talk to God about it. He made the promises to help you through your struggles. Tell Him how you feel and where you need help.
4. Learn to share your struggles and feelings in this area with other single Christians. Ask them what they do and what answers they have found for their lives. Don't push the topic under the rug in your singles group. Talk it through.
5. When you come to a place of deep conviction in your life, don't club other people with it. Try saying, "I have found this to be the best way for me to live." Leave others free to live as they choose. All you can do is share where you are and how you arrived there.

I said at the start of this chapter that this was a tough area. You won't resolve it in the next three minutes. Even after you do resolve it for yourself, you will still struggle with it a lot. Just rest assured you are not alone. *God cares!*

You were married—now you're not. Without a bed partner, it is easy to feel bereft of wholeness or completeness. The most natural desire in the world is to be held, loved, touched, and cherished. Having such feelings is certainly part of one's sexual makeup, but is it the whole story? The sex act—"making love"—is only one aspect of our sexual being. The sexual part of us experiences joy, sorrows, gains, losses, fullness, emptiness—and it is from that vulnerable storehouse of feelings and emotions that we choose to give others varying degrees of involvement as we build our sweetest experiences and memories. There is no simplistic answer. As a Christian adult it is up to you to choose how far you want to go in expressing those desires. Everyone must make that choice alone. No one can choose for you. God's Word tells us if we entrust our desires and passions to Him, He will enable us to decide correctly for ourselves. Could there possibly be a better way?

9

Sexuality and the Single Parent

From *The Single Parent* by Virginia Watts Smith

To say there is no sexual adjustment after an individual becomes single is to hide one's head in the sand, like the proverbial ostrich, and say it doesn't exist. When separation deprives an individual of this important aspect of a marriage relationship, common sense tells us there must be a void. It matters not whether it is a man or a woman, whether the marriage has been for one or fifty years, or whether the separation has come about through death, divorce, or desertion. There is a void!

The naivete of some Christians regarding sexuality, even in this so-called enlightened age, is appalling. For example, one well-educated woman approached me after reading the above statement and commented, "You know, I never realized sex was a problem for single parents."

On another occasion a Christian psychologist speaking at a singles' conference was questioned by a widower, "How does one handle his sexual drives as a single?" "Well," replied the psychologist, "you handle them the same way I do. I travel a great deal and am away from home for days, sometimes weeks, at a time. You abstain." Obviously his answer left much to be desired. Conference attendees realized his situation wasn't quite the same as theirs; he would eventually go home to his wife.

Far from being naive, however, are some Christians who become so "knowledgeable" and taken up with the world's point of view that they have conveniently forgotten or rationalized away what the Bible says about sex. Recently a Christian college graduate, since divorced and remarried, startled me by saying, "In counseling young people, I encourage them to have premarital sex. It's better to find out if you're compatible before marriage. Besides, it makes adjustment to marriage easier." This man, along with many other Christians, is allowing the world to "mold" his sexual orientation and behavior.

This type of advice, coming from a Christian, seems so less than Christian; but what can you expect when everyone, singles and single parents alike, have become prime targets for naturalistic sexual exploitation. They are being bombarded with *SEX,* sometimes with disgusting frankness. Imagine a huge billboard, placed so the public must see it blocks away, picturing a scantily clad female or a handsome, muscular male, smiling and saying, in essence, "Look like me and do the things I do, and you'll be successful, too!" Other times exploitation is so subtle that viewers are not conscious of what's happening. Advertisers know, however, that the sexual image they plant is being subconsciously stored in the viewer's mind, right where they want it!

Industry has recently discovered the potential spending power of the growing population of singles, single parents, and their children. This discovery has sparked a massive advertising program designed to reach this very special group. Now we're advised that everything from wearing snug-fitting jeans to drinking wine is the "thing to do." ("It's downright upright for a single woman to ask a man over for a drink.")

Television is also gearing more and more programs to singles and single parents. One such program entitled *Sex and the Single Parent* was, fortunately, short-lived. Books and magazines continue to discuss intimate subjects such as "The Ingenious Sex Lives of Divorced Mothers" (*Cosmopolitan,* January 1976). The author of this particular article described the unhappy sexual state of the divorced woman by saying, "Juggling a single woman's sex life with the demands of children can sometimes make you feel so incredibly hassled that all you want to do is burrow into bed and dream of running off to Guadalupe with Robert DeNiro."

Teenagers' problems are being compounded not only because of this constant emphasis on sex but also because many adults provide no clear standards regarding morality and sexual behavior. An article in *Families* magazine (May 1981) called "Teen-agers and Sex: The Price of Freedom" describes this confusion: "Some parents and educators see this reckless Sybaritism of the young as a fallout from a decade of social upheavals; women's liberation; the exploding divorce rate; the decline of parental and institutional authority; the widespread acceptance of 'living together.' The sexual revolution, they note, has also provided an unwitting new model for teens. 'There are a lot of divorced and single parents dating,' says Judith Gorbach, Director of Family Planning for the Massachusetts Department of Public Health. 'The message everywhere is sex.' "

Is it any wonder then that: (1) the number of sexually active teenagers increased by two-thirds in the seventies and that 12 million teenagers out of a total of 29 million between the ages of thirteen and nineteen had sexual intercourse or (2) that one poll, interviewing women ages eighteen and up, found that 61 percent of single and 51 percent of divorced women polled maintain that premarital sex is not necessarily immoral?

The so-called sexual freedom our society has been indulging in has not brought freedom, but rather has left its victims empty, guilty, lonely, and in bondage. Dwight Hervey Small, in his book *Christian: Celebrate Your Sexuality,* paints a vivid picture of this bondage: "Sex by itself, apart from marital bonds, stands starkly as the symbol of personal impoverishment."

Fortunately, the Christian single parent: widowed, divorced, separated, unmarried, or single adoptive, has a positive alternative to this impoverishment. Dr. M. O. Vincent, in his book *God, Sex and You,* suggests that "the Christian's moral life is the outgrowth of a new relationship to God through Jesus Christ. This personal relationship is the sure foundation of all Christian conduct." He goes on to explain to the individual who is not a Christian that "since this is the cornerstone, it is impossible to live a life ethically pleasing to God without this prior relationship. Our moral life is because we are Christian, not that our conduct makes us Christian." Now this does not suggest that Christians do not sin, but rather that the Christian has Someone to turn to for help. Jesus Christ is understanding, unconditionally loving, and forgiving, and will provide positive direction for anyone who desires it. The Christian single parent also has the Bible, which offers extensive information and guidelines to help single parents understand God's will so they may live according to His higher standards.

Since the Bible is so important to the believer, let's consider what it has to say:

God Created Us as Sexual Beings

Human sexuality was designed by God and is a God-endowed factor of personality. God created mankind in two sexes, as indicated in Mark 10:6: "But from the beginning of the creation God made them male and female" (KJV). We are therefore sexual beings with different biological drives. God, not man, created sex. It is one of God's good gifts to mankind.

God Created Us in His Image

"So God created man in his own image, in the image of God created he him . . ." Genesis 1:27 KJV tells us. Being created in the image of God, though I cannot begin to treat the theological implications, does at least speak of the supreme value of the individual to God. Human beings are not creatures whose role is merely to fulfill biological needs. God transcends biology and physiology. Now since God places such high value on us, His special creations, does it not follow that he would naturally want the best for us: spiritually, emotionally, socially, and even sexually? that He would provide guidelines for us to live our lives as He intended?

Perhaps part of our problem in making moral judgments and decisions is that we have not recognized our intrinsic value to God, nor have we understood the true meaning of being "made in the image of God." I recall counseling a young man in his early twenties. He was very withdrawn, but appeared eager to learn and become more outgoing. After one session in which we discussed the individual's importance to God, I requested that he study the principles regarding self-esteem, from the Bible, for the next few days.

When he returned, I asked, "What was helpful to you in your study this week?" His eyes sparkled as he replied, "I never knew I was valuable to anyone before."

Plato spoke of the body as a *tomb.* Paul, the New Testament apostle, in his first letter to the Corinthians (3:16) called the body a *temple.* "Know ye not that ye are the temple of God, and that the Spirit of God dwelleth in you?" (KJV). How one views one's body, tomb or temple, should make a difference in how one lives.

God Instituted Marriage at Creation

God spoke of Adam and Eve, in Genesis 2:25 KJV, as "the man and his wife." This relationship was designed for a number of very special reasons:

A. *Companionship.* Companionship was one of God's prime motives in bringing Adam and Eve together, as we discover in Genesis 2:18: "And the Lord God said, It is not good that the man should be alone; I will make him an help meet [helper, counterpart] for him" (KJV). If this important aspect of a marriage relationship were to be more strongly developed, perhaps there would be fewer divorces and separations.

B. *Sexual intimacy.* Sexual intercourse should be the fullest expression of mutual love between husband and wife, according to Proverbs 5:18, 19; 1 Corinthians 7:3–5; Hebrews 13:4, and as expressed in the beautiful love story recorded in the Song of Solomon. Genesis 2:24 defines this physical union as "they shall be one flesh" and "a man . . . shall cleave unto his wife" (KJV) *Cleave* literally means "glued together." It also suggests a lasting or permanent relationship.

C. *Procreation.* In Genesis 1:28 God commanded His new creations to "be fruitful, and multiply, and replenish the earth. . . ." In Genesis 4:1, 2 we learn that Adam and Eve did as they were instructed, "And Adam knew Eve his wife; and she conceived, and bare Cain. . . . And she again bare his brother Abel. . ." (KJV).

So you see, marriage in the beginning was characterized by loving companionship, physical intimacy, and procreation.

God Intended That Sexual Intimacies Occur Only Within the Marriage Bond

A. The seventh commandment warns, "Thou shalt not commit adultery" (Exodus 20:14 KJV).

B. Paul also gave warnings about promiscuity: ". . . Now the body is not for fornication, but for the Lord; and the Lord for the body." "Flee fornication," we are advised. For, "Every sin that a man doeth is without the body; but he that committeth fornication sinneth against his own body" (1 Corinthians 6:13, 18 KJV).

C. Promiscuity, in the Bible, is incompatible with personal holiness and is contrary to God's will: ". . .Ye ought to walk and to please God, so ye would abound more and more. . . . ye should abstain from fornication" (1 Thessalonians 4:1, 3 KJV). "But fornication and all uncleanness, . . . let it not be once named among you, as becometh saints" (Ephesians 5:3 KJV). "Set your affection on things above, not on things on the earth," and "Mortify therefore your members which are upon the earth; fornication, uncleanness, inordinate affection, evil concupiscence . . ." (Colossians 3:2, 5 KJV). (*See also* Galatians 5:16, 19–21; Genesis 12:10–20; Genesis 20:1–18; Genesis 26:6–11.)

Sexual Sins Are Not "Unpardonable"

A. Sexual sins are listed along with sins such as foolish talking, jesting, anger, wrath, malice, blasphemy, filthy communication, and lying in Colossians 3:5–9 and Ephesians 5:3, 4.

B. Jesus forgave the woman taken in adultery, in John 8:1–11. When she acknowledged Him as Lord, He declared, ". . . Neither do I condemn thee; go, and sin no more" (KJV).

C. Jesus also forgave the prostitute in Luke 7:36–50. Religious leaders were unhappy with Jesus because He allowed this woman to wash His feet with tears and then wipe them with her hair. She also kissed and anointed His feet with ointment. One of the religious leaders grumbled; "This man, if he were a prophet, would have known who and what manner of woman this is that toucheth him; for she is a sinner." Jesus confronted the unloving crowd by saying, ". . . Her sins, which are many, are forgiven; for she loved much. . . ." Turning to the prostitute, He said, "Thy sins are forgiven. . . . thy faith hath saved thee; go in peace" (KJV). Jesus made it very clear that it was her faith, not her works, that saved her.

D. David's story in 2 Samuel 11, 12 is the classic example of man's sin and God's forgiveness. David's problems began when he ". . . arose from off his bed, and walked upon the roof of the king's house: and from the roof he saw a woman washing herself; and the woman was very beautiful to look upon" (11:2 KJV). If David had only looked, he probably would have been spared a great deal of heartache. Unfortunately, "David sent and enquired after the woman" (verse 3); "David sent messengers, and took her" (verse 4); and "the woman conceived" (verse 5). But the tragedy didn't end there. David then tried to cover his sin by sending Bathsheba's husband to the front line of battle, and Uriah was killed. David suffered the consequences of his sins (as we all do). His child died. Ultimately David confessed his sin and repented, and God forgave him: "I acknowledged my sin unto thee, and mine iniquity have I not hid. I said, I will confess my transgressions unto the Lord; and thou forgavest the iniquity of my sin" (Psalms 32:5; *see also* Psalm 51).

So you see, the Bible tells us that there is forgiveness with God! Just as those in the Scriptures, though correctly referred to as sinners, found forgiveness with God, so may the single parent who has erred. The following steps will be helpful in the process of restoration:

A. *Confess your sins to God.* "If we confess our sins, he is faithful and just to forgive us our sins, and to cleanse us from all unrighteousness" (1 John 1:9 KJV).

B. *Commit your life (sex included) to God.* "Keep yourselves in the love of God . . ." (Jude 21). "Flee also youthful lusts . . ." (2 Timothy 2:22). "Likewise, reckon ye also yourselves to be dead indeed unto sin, but alive unto God, through Jesus Christ our Lord" (Romans 6:11 KJV).

C. *Control your thoughts.* John Stott, in *Your Mind Matters* (Inter-Varsity Press), contends that the "battle is nearly always won in the mind." The Bible has a great deal to say about the mind. For example: "I beseech you therefore, brethren, by the mercies of God, that ye present your bodies a living sacrifice, holy, acceptable unto God, which is your reasonable service. And be not conformed to this world: but be ye transformed by the renewing of your mind, that ye may prove what is that good, and acceptable, and perfect, will of God" (Romans 12:1, 2 KJV); ". . . bringing into captivity every thought to the obedience of Christ" (2 Corinthians 10:5); "Wherefore gird up the loins of your mind . . . As obedient children, not fashioning yourselves according to the former lusts in your ignorance" (1 Peter 1:13, 14 KJV).

D. *Count on God to help you.* Obviously God wants you, His special creation, to be successful. Paul assures you in Philippians 2:13 (TLB) that ". . . God is at work within you, helping you want to obey him, and then helping you do what he wants." You are further counseled that "there hath no temptation taken you but such as is common to man; but *God is faithful,* who will not suffer you to be tempted above that ye are able; but will with the temptation also make a way to escape, that ye may be able to bear it" (1 Corinthians 10:13 KJV, *italics added*).

E. *Contact with an empathetic church and understanding Christians will provide spiritual food and fellowship necessary for continued growth.* Fortunately, more and more Christians and organizations are becoming aware of the growing numbers of single parents and their children. They are also beginning to recognize both their potential and their need. Still, many are lagging behind and not fulfilling their obligations to the single parent. It's for sure, Christian society must consider its responsibility to help those individuals.

To be sure, Christ came not only to insure eternal life after death for the single parent who is a child of God, but also to provide that person with strength, wisdom, and power to live an abundant life here on earth. Three verses from the Bible that have been especially helpful to me when I needed an extra spiritual boost are found in Ephesians 3:20, 21 and Philippians 4:13. They read, "Now unto him that is able to do exceeding abundantly above all that we ask or think, according to the *power* that worketh in us," and, "I can do all things through Christ which strengtheneth me" (KJV).

Love is life's greatest experience. To the Christian single parent, love must be viewed, as we've learned, from a different perspective from the world's. Though we cannot totally understand God's love, it should motivate us to greater creativity throughout life—single or married, and with or without sexual intimacy.

A maturing love toward God will help us direct our thoughts to others and motivate us to action in their regard. As you channel sexual energy in a positive direction, you will not only experience a deeper commitment and love toward God and others but you will also discover you are able to use your abilities in creative ways not realized before. For example, homes and hospitals are full of sick people who also need help and encouragement. Doing the laundry; cleaning a house; going shopping or preparing a lovely meal for another person going through a crisis experience; teaching the handicapped a creative craft; reading to the aged or blind; opening your home to young people; using your car to transport people to doctors, hospitals, or meetings; sending letters and cards, or telephoning those in need are a few options for the creative use of one's energy. Or you might want to use this time in your life to develop an area you've always wanted to pursue: a hobby, music, college, teaching, sewing, carpentry, arts, crafts, or travel.

Potentially, you may discover that life is more satisfying and rewarding than you ever dreamed it could be!

Part Four

◈

Look Alive: In Tune With God

When we talk about spiritual growth, we are going into sensitive territory—our heart of hearts. When we take the journey inward we have to deal with life's deepest issues, like building of character, the value of prayer, the importance of the Scriptures, the healing of hurts, the identifying of fears, and the rewards of living an obedient life before God. It all combines to help us become fully human and fully alive. Do you know if you're fully alive? You can know—journey on.

10

Get Going, Get Growing

From *Suddenly Single* by Jim Smoke

The crisis of the death or divorce of a mate can affect a person's spiritual growth in many ways. Some who are nonspiritually oriented prior to this crisis become spiritually connected during and as a result of it. Others who were connected can become separated, disjointed, and adrift from God and growth. Still others get mad at God and blame Him for letting their tragedy happen.

One of my goals is to help you examine and evaluate your life and growth as a single-again person. A primary key to your growth is found in the spiritual area.

What Is Spiritual Growth?

In a recent conversation with a person in a singles group, the question was asked, "What is spiritual growth, and how do you really know if you are growing spiritually?" Let's try to answer that from a scriptural and practical point of view.

The Bible speaks a lot about growing. Writing to the Early Church at Ephesus, Paul says, "Rather, speaking the truth in love, we are to grow up in every way into him who is the head, into Christ" (Ephesians 4:15 RSV). Peter tells us to "grow in the grace and knowledge of our Lord and Savior Jesus Christ" (2 Peter 3:18 RSV). In his first letter, Peter states, "So put away all malice and all guile and insincerity and envy and all slander. Like newborn babes, long for the pure spiritual milk, that by it you may grow up to salvation" (1 Peter 2:1,2 RSV). Jesus, in His earthly ministry, talked repeatedly of growth and used many agrarian examples to illustrate

His points. He spoke of planting seeds, growing wheat, and harvesting crops.

A crisis can be a definite deterrent to our growth, or it can cause us to grow more than ever. I think we decide within ourselves which it will be. In his letter to the Romans, Paul says, "And we know that all things work together for good to them that love God, to them who are the called according to his purpose" (Romans 8:28 KJV). This verse does not say that everything that happens to us is good. It says that God will take everything and work it together so that the end result is good.

Losing a mate is usually not regarded as good. But out of this, God can bring good and cause tremendous growth in your life. Let's look at the ways this can happen.

Spiritual growth is believing God's promises. We build a trust level with God the same way we build a trust level with other human beings. Trust grows when it is put to the test. Our muscles develop only when they are tested, not when they lie dormant. I am always amazed when people tell me they have prayed for something and are shocked when God answers them. That's strange. He promised He would answer if we asked. We sometimes have to learn renewed trust in God by trusting Him with the little things in our lives, before we can trust Him with the bigger things. His promises are to be claimed, not just memorized.

Spiritual growth is removing fears from your life. In 2 Timothy 1:7, the writer says, "For God hath not given us the spirit of fear; but of power, and of love, and of a sound mind" (KJV). A measure of spiritual growth is stacking up your pile of fears alongside God's promises. You will find that God has the bigger pile every time.

Spiritual growth is having your hurts healed. I remember, as a little boy, running to my mother after I had fallen and scraped my knee. Mom never yelled and said I should watch more carefully where I was going. She simply bent down, cleaned off the cut, and applied a good dose of iodine. As she bandaged the cut, I was never sure whether the iodine hurt more than the wound itself. She patted me on the head and sent me back to play. The hurt subsided in a few minutes; the bandage stayed for a few days; the scar from the wound stayed forever. You should see my knees.

Healing takes place in our lives when we stop calling attention to our wounds and allow scar tissue to cover them. In the words of Dr. Robert Schuller, "We must turn our scars into stars." James tells us, "Therefore confess your sins to one another, and pray for one another, that you may be healed. The prayer of a righteous man has great power in its effects" (James 5:16 RSV).

The healing of our hurts is a sign of spiritual growth. It takes place in the emotional, psychological, and physical areas of our lives. Sometimes it has to start from the inside out. Many of our wounds are on the inside. Internal bleeding is always the most difficult to stop!

Spiritual growth is coming home. Some years ago, I got hooked on a few lines from a song by Chuck Girard. The song was called "Welcome Back." The lines said, "Welcome back to the things that you once believed in. Welcome back to what you knew was right from the start."* I meet many single-again people who, in their journey through life, are coming home to God through their crisis. The crisis of loss is not a place to hide in. It is a place to grow through. God can use your experience to bring you back into a growing place in spiritual things.

Spiritual growth is building or rebuilding your relationship with God. In his book *No Longer Strangers,* Bruce Larson says:

> A right relationship means that one has heard the good news that God says to us in Jesus Christ: "I love you as you are. I love you unconditionally. I have already given myself to you totally, and now all I ask is that you begin to respond to My Love and My commitment to you by committing to Me all of yourself that you are able to give."

That is the beginning of building a relationship with God. As in earthly relationships, there is a maintenance program to be entered upon if the relationship is to grow. I meet Christians every day who

* From the song "Welcome Back" by Chuck Girard, © 1970 Dunamis Music, 8319 Lankershim Blvd., N. Hollywood, Calif. 91605. Used by permission. International copyright secured. All rights reserved.

have had a vital encounter with God. They joined God's family. They got in the race. They just never traveled very far from the starting line. Then the chaos, the problems, the struggles of life invaded. The question "Why me?" came up. Most often the answer was, "I don't know!" Perhaps a better question is, "How do I grow through this time and come out better for it?"

Building is beginning a new relationship with God. You may need to start your life right there. Rebuilding is coming back to God and continuing the growth you once started, sometimes long ago.

Spiritual growth is coming alive! Can you remember a moment when you felt you were fully alive? It wasn't just because your heart was still beating or because something good had happened to you. It was a special experience that was hard to sum up in human language. But you knew. And you savored that moment.

Those are the mountaintops of our lives. For some of us, it may seem like the valleys outnumber the mountains 100 to 1. Spiritual growth is having a sense of being totally alive in the center of God's love.

John Powell, writing in *Fully Human, Fully Alive,* says there are five things that contribute to one's sense of being fully alive. They are: 1) to accept oneself; 2) to be oneself; 3) to forget oneself in loving; 4) to believe; 5) to belong. To these five I would add one of my own: to minister to others and to be ministered to.

You might take a minute and use the above six as a checklist or a spiritual pulse taking for yourself. Be honest. If you score low in certain areas, this is where you need to concentrate some of your growth efforts.

Jesus said in John 10:10 RSV, "... I came that they might have life, and have it abundantly." That sounds to me like being alive. For you it might mean shaking the trappings of another life and life-style from yourself and deciding to get your new life growing! All spiritual growth is measured by daily discipline. That discipline is never easy.

It's like dieting. The first hour is the hardest. The first day is a torment. The first week is agony. Then, all of a sudden, you get in the groove, build up your resistance skills, and just keep moving.

The results come slowly at first, then more noticeably. The joy and feeling of being alive comes in seeing the changes.

Then someone throws a pothole in your path in the form of a seven-layer Bavarian chocolate cake—your very favorite. Do you taste the frosting just to see what you were delivered from? Do you have a tiny piece so the cake buyer won't feel offended? Do you eat the whole thing because you deserve a reward for not eating cake for the past eight weeks? We all know that kind of experience: "a tangible temptation of the tastiest variety." It is also a turning point and a place to really measure your growth in dieting.

Steps to Spiritual Growth

There will be some potholes as you grow spiritually. As you come alive, you will find that you are able to handle them easier each time they confront you. I became a Christian when I was about twelve years old. I remember that my Sunday-school teacher and pastor placed more importance on the things I should not do now that I belonged to God than on the things I should do. My list of negatives was long and dangerous. It wasn't until many years later that I realized there was another list—shorter and, for the most part, a lot harder. That list contains things that really help a person grow in his relationship with God. I want to share them with you.

Prayer. I know, we are starting with one of the hardest ones first. It is no wonder the disciples came to Jesus and said, "Lord, teach us to pray . . ." (Luke 11:1 RSV). It's not easy to tell whether they wanted to learn for their own ends or to identify more closely with Jesus. What is implied in their request is that it is a process to be learned. Jesus responded with what is known as the Lord's Prayer. It wasn't to be the only prayer, but it was to be a model, because it summed up what God would want for us. It was a bare-bones, direct-communication prayer. It went from the theological to the practical. The Scripture doesn't say how often the disciples were to pray it. Jesus simply gave the model, and the disciples went from there.

Prayer, simply defined, is a conversation with God about anything. It is also telling God the truth about everything. All of the elements combined in building an earthly relationship go into building a relationship with God in prayer. You have to talk to Him—in twentieth-century English or whatever language you speak.

There are many ingredients that others have written about in discussing prayer that will help you. I just want to find out right here if you are talking to God these days. Are you asking for His help in all of your struggles? Do you have some problems that you feel are too big for God; others that you feel God would not be interested in hearing about? Matthew's Gospel puts it this way:

> Ask, and it will be given you; seek, and you will find; knock, and it shall be opened to you. For every one who asks receives, and he who seeks finds, and to him who knocks it will be opened."
>
> Matthew 7:7, 8 RSV

That's one of God's promises, but we have to do the asking. Prayer is a discipline. It takes time, and it is work. It is the foundation of a growing faith.

Scriptural study. The four singles crowded into my office. They were excited about the prospect of having a Bible study. We talked about dates, times, and my availability to teach. After we had agreed on these, they turned to go. I stopped them to give a homework assignment prior to the study. Their look of disbelief told me what I had suspected. They wanted me to study the Bible for them and then ladle out the truth for an hour while they listened and then went home. Real Bible study is *you* doing some work—not your preacher or your teacher, but *you.*

The shelves in Christian bookstores are overloaded with study guides, tapes, workbooks, lesson materials, resources, and commentaries. If you are serious about your own growth, you will need to buy several of the tools and get into some study for yourself.

That does not mean you can't go to a study that someone else teaches. It does mean that you can't depend on that as your only study. Just sitting in a room with ten people, reading a segment of Scripture, and then asking what each one thinks is merely a pooling of ignorance, unless you have done your homework. In order to grow, you have to study.

Second Timothy 2:15 RSV says, "Do your best to present yourself to God as one approved, a workman who has no need to be ashamed, rightly handling the word of truth." These were Paul's words to Timothy as he struggled to grow. Are you studying? Do you have the tools you need? Are you in a study group that demands something from you—or are you just being spoon-fed?

Involvement in ministry. In recent years I have watched many singles come to a meeting for the first time. They are nervous and unsure about the people, the program, the place, and themselves. Many come once and drift on to some other place. I have discovered that what brings most people back for a second or third time is a reason for them to be there. The strongest one I know is having a responsibility that can only be met by their being present. I have asked more singles to serve coffee than there are coffeepots in California. I have found that coffee servers make great group presidents, social chairmen, and retreat leaders. The beginning of ministry involvement is not as glorious as we would like to think.

Jesus' first request to some potential disciplines was simply to "follow me" (Matthew 4:19 RSV). That doesn't sound too prestigious. All ministry begins by follower involvement. The tasks come as we are equipped to handle them. I have learned that most people only support what they have a part in creating. Looking for a place to belong is one thing. Having a reason to belong anyplace is another.

Jesus slowly involved the disciplines in what He was doing. You need to become involved very slowly in any ministry opportunity. Your desire might be to jump in and take all the reins. Just take one rein. That will give you a reason to be there. Ministry involvement can go from a small group of singles to the larger church body, to mission task forces, to serving as an elder or deacon. There are hundreds of opportunities to serve. You just need one or two to start with.

Fellowship. As a child, I thought fellowship was food and drink in the church fellowship hall after a meeting. No one really explained to me that fellowship was a lot more involved than that. Fellowship is sharing your life in a supportive community that loves you.

Sometimes when we end a six-week divorce-recovery workshop, the participants ask if they can continue to meet week after week. When told the seminar is over, they usually respond by saying, "I need these people. They have become my friends. I need their support and fellowship." This kind of fellowship comes from people who share the same or similar struggles and experiences.

Fellowship is knowing you are not alone in the human condition. It's having hands to clap for you when you accomplish something. It's having hands to catch you when you falter. It's having your own private cheerleading squad. There is a kind of quiet warmth that comes from deep fellowship with other people. You can hardly explain it, but you certainly know when it's there. The Christian single-again person is in initial fellowship with Christ. That fellowship expands to every other member of the family of God.

The witness of your life. Paul was standing before King Agrippa. His life was in peril. He was speaking in his own defense. His witness was his life and what had happened to him. He was so convincing that when he concluded, Agrippa said, "In a short time you will persuade me to become a Christian" (*see* Acts 26:28 KJV). Paul was not oratorical. He was not overwhelming. He was not hyper-spiritual. He simply told the story of his conversion and his life afterward. The strongest witness anyone can give is to put his life on public display to those around him. Sharing your faith is a big part of spiritual growth. It is taking others behind the scenes to allow them to see what God is doing and has done in your life.

I was finishing a single conference some months ago on the East Coast. For some unknown reason, a strange thought popped into my head as I was wrapping up the final speaking session. A tape in my mind seemed to keep replaying the words *So what?* I concluded the session by saying, "After all that was said and shared here by so many speakers and myself, I want to close with a question: So what?"

That's what I'm asking you now: So what? What's the difference? Who will make any difference? What about your spiritual growth? Do you care enough in your own life to take some time right now and do some evaluating? No one else can do it for you. Here are some helpful suggestions:

1. Take an honest look at where you are in your spiritual growth and where you would like to be.
2. Make some positive growth plans. Write them down. Put them on your calendar.
3. Be willing to share with others how you are doing and ask their help if you feel you need it.
4. Don't be afraid to take risks and make new commitments to grow.
5. Discover what spiritual gifts you have and find a place to utilize them.
6. Learn to feel yourself spiritually.
7. Watch out for people who set themselves up as spiritual gurus.
8. Don't let others dictate your growth patterns. Spiritual growth is not a race—it's a journey. You don't need to be more "spiritual" than someone else.

My prayer for you is that as you are suddenly single again, you are growing spiritually.

Spiritually mature—any believer covets the label. Yes, *covets,* but not in the sense of the Tenth Commandment, which warns against wanting something that belongs to your neighbor. You can't take spiritual maturity from anyone. It is between you and God. It's there for the having—if you want it badly enough.

11

Becoming Spiritually Mature

From *Getting Started* by Gary R. Collins

Recently, I celebrated an anniversary. It was a quiet celebration. There were no banners, gifts, cards, parades, or fireworks. It wasn't mentioned in the newspaper or on the TV news. Twenty years earlier the president of Purdue University had signed a diploma that gave me a doctorate in psychology.

It had taken a lot of work for me to reach that milestone. I was never a strong student. It was a combination of youthful determination, dogged persistence, and the patience of a small army of teachers that moved me from kindergarten to graduate school and on to the day when I finally earned the right to call myself a psychologist.

In the last two decades, I have read many criticisms of my profession. Some seem to be biased and inaccurate, but others have been well researched and thought-provoking. Around the time of my anniversary, for example, a clinical psychologist named Bernie Zilbergeld published an insight critique of counseling (*The Shrinking of America: Myths of Psychological Change*) and argued that therapy is neither as needed nor as effective as we might like to believe.

According to Dr. Zilbergeld, many people in America accept some assumptions about life that aren't necessarily true. We conclude, for example, that the world is best understood in psychological terms, that people are not okay as they are, that everyone needs and can benefit from therapy, that we have a right to happiness, that all problems can be solved, and that psychology is the best route to personal fulfillment. Perhaps it isn't surprising that America has been called the "world capital of psychological-

mindedness and therapeutic endeavor." E. G. Boring once pre-
dicted that the day could come when "there will be more psycholo-
gists than people in this country."

I mention all of this because it seems that some of my fellow
Christians have followed our society into thinking that the hope for
our generation is found in psychology. Zilbergeld titled his book
The Shrinking of America but I wonder if there hasn't also been a
"shrinking of the church." Pastoral counseling, marriage enrich-
ment, possibility thinking, personal enhancement, transparency development, self-help groups, stress- and time-management
seminars, psychologically based fund-raising and advertising cam-
paigns—these and a number of other psychological influences have
slipped into the local congregation. Such trends are not necessarily
bad. Since becoming a psychologist, I have encouraged many of
them myself. But even good and useful psychological ideas can distract from a basic Christian assumption: Our hope is in the Lord
(Psalms 146:5).

When Simon Peter wrote his second epistle, influences more dangerous than psychology were seeping into the church and distracting the early believers from sound doctrine. After reminding the
readers of God's righteousness, grace, peace, and power, the epistle
writer made the remarkable statement that God has given us everything we need to live a good life (2 Peter 1:1–4). Christian living is
not meant to be what someone has called "an initial spasm followed
by a chronic inertia." Instead, we are to accept what God has promised and then make diligent and consistent effort to live lives that
are characterized by faith, goodness, knowledge, self-control, perse-
verance, godliness, kindness, and love (2 Peter 1:5–9).

Such thinking is foreign both to contemporary psychology and to
the daily lives of most young (and older) adults in our society. The
people with whom Christians work, study, relax, do business, and
live, often have values that are far removed from the teachings of
the Bible. This presents most of us with some strong dilemmas. How
can we live in ways that are vocationally successful and pleasing
to Christ when we are part of a society that rejects Christian
principles?

Several young adults have expressed their concerns about these issues in seminars I have taught:

As a Christian, how do I relate to my non-Christian friends and family members? What are my responsibilities?

As life gets busier for me, how can I find time to read the Bible and pray?

Often I am unsure about my beliefs. My Christian walk is always going up and down. Is this normal?

How do I overcome the "keeping up with the Joneses" philosophy? I'm always worrying about impressing others with material things to show how successful I have been. What does God say about this? How can I quit comparing myself with others?

It isn't easy for me to turn my burdens over to the Lord and then to leave them with Him. Instead, I worry a lot. How can I handle this spiritual struggle?

How does one keep his eyes on Christ and still have the drive and time to succeed in business? How can I be a good Christian example in the business world?

How do I fit in the church when they think I am too young and inexperienced to do anything?

It's hard for me to be patient and to trust God to bring my dreams and aspirations together.

How do I bring Christ into my profession without pushing my beliefs onto others? My profession considers that unethical.

In this chapter we will look at some of these issues as they relate to the Christian's professional life. We will consider how faith in Christ can influence our personal and prayer lives. The place to start, however, is with a look at our private lives.

The Christian's Private Life

Long before Christ was born, God spoke to a man named Abraham and told him to move. There were no moving companies to help the man's family relocate, and at that point they didn't even know where they would be going. Nevertheless, without hesitation, Abraham obeyed.

This was the story of his life. Consistently he trusted the Lord and followed His commands, even when the instructions seemed strange and illogical. When God told the old man to sacrifice his only son, for example, Abraham decided immediately to obey. The young boy was placed on the altar until God stopped the proceedings and provided a sacrificial lamb instead. In accordance with the custom of that time and country, Abraham gave a name to the place where this happened. He called it *Jehovah-jireh*. The words mean "The Lord will provide" (Hebrews 11:8–19).

I've often thought about this in my own life. God has promised to provide all that we need, but do I really believe He will do this? (Philippians 4:19). I have no doubt that He *can* provide; but sometimes, when there are important decisions to be made or when my family has special financial needs, doubt raises its ugly head and I wonder if He *will* provide as He has promised.

I suspect my thinking is not unique. It is difficult to believe that God will provide the resources, wisdom, patience, and opportunities we need to get through this life. We are part of a culture that praises individual drive, planning, initiative, and creativity. We are not used to seeking divine guidance before we forge ahead with our plans. Even Christians admire the "self-made person," and we aren't inclined to give much thought to the fact that everything we have and do depends on God.

Philip Yancey is one of my favorite writers, not only because of his way with words but also because of his penetrating insights. "Self-sufficiency is the most fatal sin because it pulls us, as if by a magnet, from God," he wrote in *Open Windows*.

> Tensions and anxieties flame within me the moment I forget I am living my life for the one-man audience of Christ and slip into living my life to assert myself in a competitive world.
>
> Previously, my main motivation in life was to do a painting of myself, filled with bright colors and profound insights, so that all who looked upon it would be impressed. Now, however, I find

that my role is to be a mirror, to brightly reflect the image of God through me. Or perhaps the metaphor of stained glass would serve better, for, after all, God will illuminate through my personality and body. . . .

I no longer find my identity in my apartness from the rest of the world. Now, I find it in my sameness. I am exactly the same as everyone in the world in terms of my standing before God—I am a sinner. . . .

I cannot imagine a more difficult stumbling block in Christianity. It is relatively easy to inspire people with the Christian ethic of love. . . . But every mechanism of self-protection within me cries out against this painful, renouncing step of identifying myself as a sinner.

If there could be no hope beyond this realization, our lives would be futile and in true existential despair. But God, in His wisdom, sent Jesus Christ to pay for our sins. We are not forced to accept or to believe that this really happened; humans, at their peril, are free to reject Christ. But if we confess our sin and acknowledge that Jesus is Lord, He forgives, and completely changes our lives (1 John 1:9).

Yancey has commented on the effects of this decision:

After going through the humiliating act of losing myself by letting go of that protective pride, I suddenly find myself with a new identity—the exalted state that Paul describes as "in-Christness." No longer must I defend my thoughts, my values, my actions. I trade those in for the identity I am given as a son of God. . . .

My sense of competition quickly fades. No longer do I have to bristle through life, racking up points to prove myself. My role has ideally become to prove God, to live in such a way that people around me recognize Jesus and his love, not the other set of qualities which separate me from the world. I have found this process to be healthy, relaxing, and wholly good.

The writer of those words has a life that is different, not only because he has made a complete commitment to Christ but also because there has been a change in his private thinking.

Have you ever heard it said that "as a man thinks, so he is"? If we could really know how another person thinks, we would have an accurate picture of what that person is like.

Thinking is part of our private lives. The only ones who really know what or how I think are God, me, and anyone to whom I choose to reveal my thoughts. Nevertheless, if my thinking tends to be critical, competitive, or complacent, that will mold my actions, color my emotions, and shape my personality. If, in contrast, I have a positive, grateful outlook on life, or if I believe, like Abraham, that the Lord will always provide, these ideas also influence me significantly.

The committed and maturing Christian seeks to think in ways that would please Christ (1 Corinthians 2:16). Of course our minds wander and our perspectives get distorted, but life is healthier and less pressured if our private thinking is consistent with biblical teaching. How powerful are the inspired words of Paul: "Whatever is true, whatever is honorable, whatever is right, whatever is pure, whatever is lovely, whatever is of good repute, if there is any excellence and if anything worthy of praise, let your mind dwell on these things" (Philippians 4:8 NASB). Such thinking has a positive influence on us psychologically, and it spills over to influence the ways in which we live our personal lives.

The Christian's Personal Life

A twenty-four-year-old woman recently called a Christian radio station to participate in a talk show. She reported that she was a believer, divorced from her first husband, and living with a man to whom she was not married. She admitted that her life-style was not consistent with biblical teachings and expressed some concern that her male friend was not a believer.

"Have you talked with him about Christ or told him about your beliefs?" the program host asked.

"No," the caller responded. "I believe religious belief is a private matter. It's just between God and me. It is too personal to talk about with someone else."

At the midpoint of this century, respected Harvard psychologist Gordon W. Allport wrote in *The Individual and His Religion* that sex and religion seemed to have reversed their positions. In earlier decades we talked openly about our beliefs, but reserved sexual comments and behavior for the bedroom. Now sex is discussed freely, but we are embarrassed to say much about our beliefs or to let them influence our daily actions.

Such an attitude would have been unthinkable in the early church. The first Christians made more than an intellectual commitment to Christ. They determined to let Him mold their thinking, their marriages, their work, their values, and their futures. In short, Christ influenced their whole lives.

Are Christians any different today? Does Christ make a practical difference in your personal life, or in mine? To answer these questions, we must give some thought to the issue of life-styles.

Suppose somebody could follow you around for a few weeks and see how you related to other people, spent your time or money, and reacted to events in your environment. Before long, your follower would notice that you tend to react to situations in similar ways. These similarities are what we mean by life-style. According to Alfred Adler, the man who first used the word, a *life-style* is "a person's unique and characteristic pattern of relating to his world and environment."

After observing counselees for several years, psychologist Emery Nester concluded that a healthy life-style has five features. (These are discussed in *Depression* by Don Baker and Emery Nester.)

First, there must be firm personal commitments. If you are committed to a person or to a cause, you do not allow danger, discouragement, or inconvenience to distract you. Your thinking and your actions are directed toward the object of commitment, and you keep that object clearly in mind.

If we are really committed to following Jesus Christ, that will make a practical difference in our life-styles. The example of Abraham is relevant once again.

Dr. Nester believes that depression is especially common among young adults. He describes people under thirty as "the generation of depressives," and goes on to suggest that *one* of the reasons for depression is that people don't have any commitments. What about you?

A second feature of the healthy life-style is for one to have an adequate philosophy of life. You might want to ask yourself three questions. In your opinion, what is real? What is true? What is good? It could be helpful to write down your answers.

This is a difficult assignment, but what you write is a good indication of your philosophy of life. That philosophy influences how you live.

A willingness to admit that we are human is a third feature of the healthy life-style. Perhaps there is a perfectionistic streak in all of us. We don't like to admit that we are weak or that we "goof." Christians are reluctant to acknowledge that they lust or are greedy.

It is natural to be disappointed, to feel angry, to cry or laugh, to make mistakes or to think negative thoughts. We might not like some of these human characteristics, and we might have difficulty changing, especially for the better, but to admit our humanness is to move toward greater spiritual and psychological health. To admit our humanness also brings a more relaxed and less hectic life-style.

Fourth, the healthy life-style is characterized by an inner sense of direction. When a person has clear goals in life it is easy to feel a sense of direction, but what if you don't yet have clear goals? Must you flounder?

Not if you are a Christian. According to the Bible, God's Holy Spirit lives within the believer and guides our lives so that our behavior is more Christlike (1 Corinthians 6:19). None of us needs to be swayed by circumstances or pushed about by the actions of others. We are not like mules who need to be led in a mindless way. "I will instruct you," said the Lord. "I will counsel you and watch over you" (Psalms 32:8,9 NIV). Such inner guidance gives us a sense of direction.

Finally, people with healthy life-styles are able to accept the fact that they are unique. Sometimes we resent our idiosyncrasies and complain because we are not like others whom we admire. But we can be glad that, like snowflakes, every one of us has been made as a unique creation of God. We have special gifts, abilities, and personalities. All of these help to mold our life-styles. All have a bearing on our vocational or professional lives.

The Christian's Professional Life

I know a nurse who used to work in the office of a local private practitioner. The doctor is a Christian, an active church member, and a man who, in his medical work, adamantly refuses to mention Christ or to let his beliefs be known to the patients. The doctor's employees have been told that it is unethical to mention religion in the office or hospital room. Frustrated over this muzzling policy, my nurse friend recently quit her job.

Most professional people would agree, I suspect, that it is not appropriate to be preaching when we should be providing medical, psychological, dental, or other professional services. I once read of a physician who covered his waiting room with wallpaper printed with Bible verses. He was criticized, even by his fellow believers, and rightly so. But for Christians, isn't it also unethical, if not blatantly sinful, to pretend that Christ has no relevance to the needs of patients? When people are facing crises and even death, isn't it wrong to erect a rigid barrier between our professional mannerisms and our knowledge of the Gospel message?

The question goes far beyond medical practice. Can we really hope to mature spiritually or claim to be serving Christ obediently if we divorce our beliefs from our businesses? If we believe that Christ is to be Lord of our lives, He must be Lord of our vocations. How, then, can we serve Him effectively at work without alienating our employers and fellow workers or without taking advantage of our clients and employees?

The Book of Colossians gives a partial answer: "Whatever you do, work at it with all your heart, as working for the Lord, not for men. . . . It is the Lord Christ you are serving" (Colossians 4:23, 24 NIV). Here again is an emphasis on attitudes and ways of thinking. As we work, we must keep in mind that in everything we are serving the Lord. That means that we will strive to be honest, industrious, and effective in our work. We might not have opportunity to say much about our faith, but in time people will know we are different because of our diligence and dedication to competence. Here is a practical example of letting our "light" shine before others so they can see our "good works" and honor the Father who is in heaven (Matthew 5:16).

In the little New Testament Book of Titus, we read about the qualifications of church leaders (Titus 1:6–9). Presumably these standards were intended to be high. Not everyone could pass the test. These requirements are specific, however, and they give goals that could guide all of us in our vocations.

In life and work, let us strive to be

- blameless: people whose actions are above reproach
- sensitive to our family needs
- not troublemakers, overbearing, insensitive, self-willed, quick-tempered, violent, greedy people
- individuals who are hospitable, loving what is good, self-controlled, fair, devout, disciplined and "not addicted" to alcohol
- committed to biblical teaching
- inclined to encourage others, to state what we believe, and to refute the theological error

If we believe that the Holy Spirit guides our lives, we can expect that he will help us develop these traits and give us guidance in terms of when to express our faith verbally and when to keep quiet but give a silent witness.

As Christians, we respect those people who disagree with our beliefs. It *is* unethical to force theology on our fellow workers and business or professional associates, but the Great Commission forbids us to keep silent forever. I disagree with the talk-show caller who thinks religion is so personal that we don't even mention it to our roommates. In our era of change and uncertainty, many people are searching for an anchor of stability and hope. Even in a nation that claims to be Christian, many have never heard the Gospel. We have a responsibility to share the Good News, but not in a stilted, stereotyped, or insensitive way. Ask God to prepare minds—yours and others. Then we can trust Him to guide our conversations so that "witnessing" becomes as natural as talking about our interests or neighborhood activities.

Recently I had lunch with an air force chaplain who described some of the challenges of sharing and keeping one's faith alive in a military setting. He talked of competition, of the need to be noticed by one's superiors, of the importance of hiding problems or insecurities least these become known and used as evidence to block a promotion. What my friend sees in the military permeates civilian life as well. It is professional suicide to be honest or humble. People who don't show drive and competition don't get promotions. In many places, apparently including doctors' offices and military bases, it can be a vocational disadvantage to even mention one's beliefs.

There is no easy way out of these dilemmas. There are no set rules concerning how we bring our faith into our vocations. We can only be willing to have God use us. In time He will—sometimes even without our awareness.

What we do need is an awareness of who God is and what he wants for His children. We can't bring God into our professional lives unless He is an integrated part of our personal lives. This brings us to the issue of prayer.

The Christian's Prayer Life

Tucked in the shelves of my bookcase are perhaps a dozen books describing "contemporary" college students. I've collected these volumes over the years and have noticed how the descriptions of students have changed. There was a time when religion was not a popular subject on campus. Later there arose a student generation that had great interest in the Jesus movement and another was fascinated with the idea of being "born again." More recently, cults have captured student minds, and universities have seen an explosion of interest in religion courses. Arthur Levine says, in *When Dreams and Heroes Died: A Portrait of Today's College Student,* that religious commitment among students is dropping, that college-age adults are tired of the traditional church, but that parachurch organizations are alive and active. He found that students are pessimistic about the country but optimistic about their personal futures. In preparing for the years ahead, they are like people "going first class on the Titanic."

Do you see any of these attitudes in yourself or in your friends? Are there young adults who sail through life, caught up in its pleasures and successes, but with little awareness of the dangers or obstacles that might lurk ahead? In building lives and careers, have we forgotten the Creator, who is available like a pilot, to help us navigate through life? Has religion for many people become little more than a three-credit college course?

Not long ago, I reached a new stage in parenthood. My eldest daughter, who had just turned sixteen and finally was in possession of a driver's license, drove off by herself to a meeting in another town. I had watched her drive many times before. She had shown that she was a good driver, and I knew she would be careful. But she was also inexperienced, and less aware of the dangers than her slightly nervous father, who watched as the car backed out of the driveway.

After she left that morning, I wondered if God looks at His children in similar ways. We have only limited experience with life and spiritual things. As we move on this journey through life, we could make costly and dangerous errors in judgment. In a country where interest in God and spiritual things keeps changing, we could move far away from the One who created us. We could build values and develop life-styles that give immediate pleasure but ultimately are self-defeating.

How do we avoid this? We have all heard about stress-management skills, communication skills, child-rearing skills, life-planning skills, and time-management skills—to mention a few. Is it possible that we can also develop spiritual-growth skills? Just as consistent practicing is needed to improve the pianist's musical skills and abilities, so consistent time with the Lord—"practicing the presence of God," to use Brother Lawrence's term—is a prerequisite for spiritual growth.

Over the centuries, thousands of books have been written to give instructions on spiritual skills and growth. Go to any library or Christian bookstore and you will find books on prayer, Bible study, and personal religious devotions. Some of these are very helpful, although they are far too detailed to be summarized here. Instead, let us look briefly at the spiritual actions of Jesus. How did He relate to His heavenly Father?

First, Jesus prayed. Prayer was at the center of His life. He prayed in the temple. He prayed alone. He prayed as He went about His daily activities. He prayed before meals, before making decisions, before doing God's work, and before facing crises. He who was the Son of God knew that prayer was crucial. Can it be any less important for His followers? If we want spiritual power and growth, we have no alternative but to take time to communicate with God in prayer.

Prayer is the offering to God of our praise and desires. It involves adoration, honest confession, the giving of thanks, the expressing of our commitment to Him, and the sharing of our petitions. Prayer, it has been suggested by John E. Gardner, author of *Personal Religious Disciplines,* "should concern itself less and less with the sort of petition that says 'give me, give me.' Such prayers will recede as they are replaced by earnest petition that God will grant wisdom and strength with which the servant may meet his needs and measure up to the high calling of God."

Second, in addition to the importance of prayer, it is clear that the spirituality of Jesus was related to His knowledge of the Scriptures. How easy it is to hear sermons and read *about* God, while we fail to spend time listening directly *to* God. He speaks to us in a variety of ways, including through books and sermons, but nothing is clearer than the message that comes directly through a consistent study of the Bible.

Bible study can be done in different ways: by reading and meditating, by taking notes, by small group discussion with other Christians, by using Bible study guides, by memorizing verses. Like me, you may have used them all, and more. Probably you realize that a method may work well for one person and not for another. We each have times and places for Bible reading which suit us best.

Each of us may also find that it is easy to get distracted and to put off spending time with God. Somehow other pressing activities always seem to be more important than times of meditation. Even dedicated Christians find that it is easy to push God into the background and to hurry through our days giving lip service, but little time or thought to the Lord. Rarely do we face the fact that spiritual growth only comes to those who are disciplined enough to spend time with God—time alone and time spent at worship in the company of other believers.

Back in graduate school, before they gave me that psychology degree, I decided to spend at least a brief time alone with God each day, and to be consistent in Sunday worship. Little interfered with this decision, although I was, and am, constantly tempted to push God aside because of other demands. In our own strength it is difficult, perhaps impossible, to walk consistently with God. But the Holy Spirit helps us, not only to pray and to meditate, but to understand and apply the truths of Scripture.

A group of people once came to engage Jesus in a theological debate. Far from having a casual interest in religion, these people were the professional theologians of their day. They were spiritual leaders, but Jesus recognized that they were also spiritually ignorant and spiritually dead. He stated the reason for this in one powerful sentence.

"You are in error because you do not know the scriptures or the power of God" (Matthew 22:29 NIV).

What an indictment. Could the same be said of you or of me? The way to know the Scriptures and the power of God is to spend time in prayer and in reading God's Word.

Jesus knew this, but he was not a recluse who lived a contemplative life far removed from the daily pressures and politics of his society. Jesus prayed. Jesus knew the Scriptures. And Jesus reached out to others.

Serving, caring, encouraging, sharing, helping—these are all part of the Christian message. There is no such thing as a self-centered Christianity. Contemplation and compassion, personal prayer and practical people-helping, quiet meditation and active outreach— these are like two sides of a coin. There can't be real Christian growth without both personal spiritual discipline and willing public service.

For many people, it seems that religion is largely irrelevant to the modern world. There is little time for God, little recognition that He is needed, little interest in His teaching, and almost no inclination to obey His commandments.

Looking back over my two decades as a psychologist, I have been impressed with two conclusions. First, modern psychology can help us to live more effectively, to cope with problems, and to mature as individuals. Much of psychology may be a gift from God to help us with the pressures of living.

But (this is my second conclusion) psychology, like every other area of study, is limited when it fails to recognize the power of God. It is He who gives everything that we need "for life and godliness" (2 Peter 1:3 NIV). The psychology in this and other books can be helpful, but true fulfillment, personal growth, and spiritual maturity come only when we place our lives under God's control and trust Him to guide in the day-to-day activities of moving through adulthood.

How to Start a Bible Study Group

From *Today's Christian Woman* Magazine

November/December 1983

by Kelsey Menehan

Bible study groups are becoming increasingly popular—and for good reasons. They combine fellowship with a chance to learn more about the Bible and they can be organized and run almost anywhere by anyone. If you use your common sense in starting a group, you won't go far wrong, but it can't hurt to learn from the experience of others. Here are the five tips most frequently mentioned by women who've started and led groups.

Start with a small planning group. It's easier to set goals with five people than with twenty-five. Before recruiting, sit down with a small group of friends and decide what kind of study you want, who you want to invite, and what materials to use.

You should also decide the approach the group will take. Possibilities range from a lecture to a free-flowing sharing of ideas or a structured discussion.

Evaluate materials carefully. Most groups use a study guide to structure the discussion, and there is a wealth of this kind of material. A good set of study questions will help the group notice the specific details of the passage, understand the author's main point, and apply that point to their own lives in a personal, practical way.

Work out administrative details in advance. The most critical of these details is baby-sitting. The availability of a baby-sitter can determine the success or failure of a group. Leaders stress that children should not be kept in the same home where the study group meets. Another important idea is to have meeting places lined up for the first few sessions.

Establish clear ground rules. Old-timers stress the importance of establishing starting and ending times and sticking to them. The most common format is ten minutes of initial sharing, an hour for the study, ten minutes for additional sharing, and ten to fifteen minutes for praying together. Participants should agree to attend a specific number of meetings to give the experiment a chance and should also prepare the lesson material.

Don't expect perfection. People will move in and out of the group. In some cases they will leave regretfully because of a move or other obligation. But some women will decide that the group simply is not right for them and look elsewhere. People want different things from Bible study groups, and as long as your group is meeting needs, don't expect to please the entire world.

Epilogue

From *Changepoints* by Joyce Landorf

Don't ever listen or take to heart the voices around you that would shout—"God doesn't care about you. Who are you to Him? How can He be involved in the tiny details of your life when he has billions of people to look after?"

We have, carefully preserved, for *all* of us, the marvelous words of Psalm 121. Read these words slowly and inject them into the bloodstream of mind, body and soul:

"He will never let me stumble, slip or fall. For He is always watching, never sleeping.... He keeps his eye upon you as you come and go, and always guards you" (Psalms 121:3, 4, 8 TLB).

Our God never sleeps, and His eyes are always watching and guarding us. Astounding!

I remember when the whole Landorf family took our granddaughter, April Joy, on her first trip to Disneyland. She was just two-and-a-half years old, but the timing was *perfect* for the experience. At one point during the afternoon, she got to meet (and kiss) Minnie and Mickey Mouse. The slides we took of her show unrestrained joy all over her angelic little face. That meeting was the high point of her whole two-and-a-half years. She laughed and enjoyed many things that day, but *nothing* came up to the thrill of touching and talking with Disney's most famous characters. Nothing until the evening parade, that is.

There must have been several thousand people jammed into the Main Street area for the fantastic electric parade of floats that night.

April was in her father's arms so she could see the multitude of tiny, sparkling lights on each float. The number of floats seemed endless, and the music all over the park was simply incredible. All the Disney characters were there, riding these electrical master-pieces. Snow White and her Seven Dwarfs were waving and smiling at the people as they came by ... Goofy, Donald Duck, Pinocchio ... and then suddenly there was this enormous float with Mickey and Minnie Mouse sitting way up on top. They were waving to everybody, the music was blaring, balloons were being released, the crowd was cheering and applauding, and in that moment, April took her father's chin in her hand. She looked into his face and, her blue eyes round with wonder, she said awesomely. "He sees me! Mickey sees me. Minnie sees me! She's waving *at me!* He *sees me!*"

Darling single person, standing in the cheering, waving, ap-plauding crowd—look up! God never sleeps. He sees you! He sees you!

He really does, and He's not a cartoon, a mythical invention of someone's imaginative mind, but the true-living and real God.

The very same God who, long before the foundations of the world were laid, chose you.

He sees you—oh, yes—and you are loved! Continue your soloing. Do it in all joy, for He sees you, and He has a plan you can trust!